7 Secrets to Spiritual Success

7 SECRETS TO SPIRITUAL SUCCESS

WOOD KROLL

Multnomah®Publishers *Sisters, Oregon*

7 SECRETS TO SPIRITUAL SUCCESS

published by Multnomah Publishers, Inc.
© 2000 by Woodrow Kroll

International Standard Book Number: 1-57673-664-4

Cover illustration by Mark Ttomalty/Masterfile
Design by David Uttley Design

Scripture quotations are from:
The Holy Bible, New King James Version © 1984 by Thomas Nelson, Inc.

Also quoted:
The Holy Bible, New International Version (NIV)
© 1973, 1984 by International Bible Society,
used by permission of Zondervan Publishing House

Multnomah is a trademark of Multnomah Publishers, Inc., and
is registered in the U.S. Patent and Trademark Office.

The colophon is a trademark of Multnomah Publishers, Inc.

Printed in the United States of America

For information:

MULTNOMAH PUBLISHERS, INC.
POST OFFICE BOX 1720
SISTERS, OREGON 97759

00 01 02 03 04 05 — 10 9 8 7 6 5 4 3 2 1 0

CONTENTS

To Linda, my wife and spiritual partner since 1965

and a significant influence on my discovery

of these seven secrets to spiritual success.

ACKNOWLEDGMENTS

Books don't just happen. They are the product of the minds and skills of many people, and I gratefully acknowledge and express my genuine appreciation to those who have contributed in a significant way to this one:

- to my wife, Linda, for her constant encouragement in writing and for her patience in waiting when I didn't leave my study immediately when called for dinner.

- to my mentors and friends who, over half a century, have contributed to my own understanding of spiritual growth and have provided excellent examples of how success is achievable.

- to all the members of my *Back to the Bible* team, especially Tom Schindler, my executive vice president, who have shouldered more than their share of my responsibilities while I gave long hours to this project.

- to my administrative assistant, Cathy Strate, who managed so well to insure that I had blocks of time to write and that all the pieces of this puzzle were put together properly.

- to my good friend and research assistant, Allen Bean, who was of immense help to me in gathering supportive materials and running down details.

- to the many people I have talked with and interviewed whose stories have contributed to illustrating the seven secrets to spiritual success.

- and, of course, to the team at Multnomah Publishers, who have insured that my thoughts and experiences have been communicated to you in an attractive and readable form. I am deeply grateful to Don Jacobson, president and publisher; Kevin Marks, executive vice president; Bill Jensen, vice president of editorial; Jeff Pederson, vice president of marketing; Jay Echternach, vice president of sales; Eric Weber, vice president of production; Steve Curley, design communications coordinator; and especially to Keith Wall, senior editor.

LAUNCHING OUT ON THE JOURNEY

"Houston, we have a problem."
ASTRONAUT JIM LOVELL

On April 11, 1970, the third planned lunar landing mission blasted off from Cape Canaveral with Jim Lovell, John Swigert, and Fred Haise aboard. At launch time, everything was good to go.

But two days later and 205,000 miles from earth, Apollo 13 experienced a rupture in the fuel-cell oxygen tank of the service module. The resulting explosion caused the spacecraft to lose its oxygen, electrical power, and other systems, including its capability to perform an abort maneuver for a direct return to earth. The quick-thinking crew had only one chance for survival. They hurriedly moved to the lunar module, which became their lifeboat in space. But the lunar module was designed for a moon landing; it had no heatshield, so it could not be used for reentry into the earth's atmosphere. Just before reentry, however, the three astronauts eased their way back into the crippled command module and splashed down safely in the Pacific Ocean on April 17, 1970, more than five days after the launch. NASA and the world breathed a collective sigh of relief.

Do you remember where you were during the drama of Apollo 13? It was one of those freeze-frame moments—like when President John Kennedy was assassinated or students were being gunned down at Columbine High. I was in France, a student at the University of Strasbourg, finishing up my final year of seminary. Like everyone else, I was riveted to the radio, eager to snatch any encouraging news about the fate of the three American astronauts. I remember thinking to myself, *How horrible to be on such an exciting journey and yet one so filled with difficulty and danger.*

But life is like that. It's not so unusual. In fact, you and I are on a journey filled with difficulties and dangers no less threatening than those faced by the crew of Apollo 13. Ours, however, is a spiritual journey, not a journey to the moon. Nevertheless, the ride is not always a smooth one. To be successful on our spiritual journey, we will have to be as resourceful as those astronauts were and pay close attention to informed instruction like the Apollo 13 crew received from Houston.

THE BEGINNING OF A JOYOUS JOURNEY

My own spiritual journey was launched when I was five years old. It began one cold winter night in a tiny country church. My father was pastor of the church, and when I say tiny I mean *tiny*. A hundred people would have meant standing room only. The church had invited a children's evangelist to hold a crusade. Night after night he did some magic tricks, and after he got our attention, he would tell us about Jesus and God's love for us.

It was early March. There was half a foot of snow on the ground, and when the sun went down each evening, the temperature plummeted just as rapidly. Fortunately, this one-room church had a big potbellied stove in the middle of the room. A deacon would come in each evening and fire up that stove with wood and coal. When the service began, the temperature in the church could not have been more than sixty degrees. But by the time the service ended, it felt like a hundred and ten degrees. So hot was that stove that the church had removed the first pew behind it—first-row dwellers would have roasted. And the second wooden pew had the paint blistered off it.

On the night after telling the old gospel story, the evangelist invited anyone who wanted to trust Christ as Savior to come forward and meet him at the front. Though I was only five, I clearly understood my need for a Savior and that Jesus was the only Savior this world would ever have. I made my way to the front of the church. The evangelist and I knelt at that blistered pew, and when he talked about the fires of hell, I knew exactly what he was talking about. Then and there my spiritual journey began, and what a joy it has been to walk with the Lord ever since.

SUCCESS IS MORE LIKELY THAN FAILURE

But like the Apollo 13 flight, journeys that are joyous are often dangerous as well. Often we encounter unexpected obstacles. In fact, on the spiritual journey it's easy to stumble, stall, or enter a spiritual cul-de-sac and get sidetracked. We've all been there, done that. But if you think you've developed a penchant at Apollo 13-like disasters in your spiritual journey, I have good news. It doesn't have to be that way. Spiritual success is just as achievable as failure.

Apollo 13 wasn't the only mission to the moon. The program included twelve manned missions: two into earth's orbit (Apollo 7 and 9); two into lunar orbit (Apollo 8 and 10); three lunar landing missions (Apollo 11, 12, and 14); and three lunar exploration missions (Apollo 15, 16, and 17), which involved extended stays on the moon's surface and more in-depth scientific research.[1] NASA's manned space flight record is remarkably successful. That's because they have a manual, they follow procedures, and they take precautions. Success doesn't just happen; but when success is planned, it is frequently achieved.

If you know God's secrets, spiritual success will be more likely than failure, too. In the pages that follow, there are no magical formulas, no quick fixes to spiritual malfunctions, no thirty-day guarantees. What you will find is much better. You will discover how to be spiritually successful by positioning your life with God's global positioning system. You will discover what the Bible has to say about the true nature of success. You will discover the real source of joy and genuine happiness, because following God's guidelines for living will dramatically reduce your potential for failure.

"HEAVEN, WE HAVE A PROBLEM"

I can see it now. You're cruising along in your spiritual life when all of a sudden you have the equivalent of a rupture in your fuel-cell oxygen tank. You quickly fire off a prayer and say, "Heaven, we have a problem." Not to worry. God is better than NASA at fixing problems. Besides, He has already addressed many of the problems you will encounter when He revealed His spiritual success plan in His Word. All you have to do is know what His secrets are, take them seriously, and enjoy the result. Isn't it time you tasted the thrill of victory?

The journey from this moment to eternity ought to be more thrilling than the journey from earth to the moon. But when problems disrupt the journey, we need the right answers and a quick response time. In 7 Secrets to Spiritual Success you'll discover the right answers. The response time is up to you.

CHARTING A COURSE FOR SUCCESS

Anyone who has walked with God for a while or anyone who has read John Bunyan's classic allegory *Pilgrim's Progress* knows that the Christian life is a journey. It has a definite starting place and a definite goal. Our spiritual journey begins when we receive Jesus Christ as Savior, as I did on that wintry night at age five. When we begin our pilgrimage with God, He is suddenly no longer a distant deity in a galaxy far, far away. He is right here with us; we can almost touch Him. When we turn our life over to God, old things pass away, and all things become new.

Our journey of faith is not static but dynamic. We are constantly on the move, heading somewhere. The ultimate goal of this journey is heaven and an eternal relationship with God. But between our new birth and our new home, our walk of faith seldom follows a smooth, predictable trajectory. In fact, I often liken the Christian life to a game of golf. Sometimes the game goes quickly; sometimes it drags on. Sometimes the weather is ideal; sometimes it is horrible. Sometimes you play to your full potential; sometimes you muddle through. Sometimes you enjoy the game; sometimes it is maddening.

As with any good round of golf, success on our spiritual journey comes in knowing the purpose of the game and how to make the shots so that, as much as possible, you stay out of the rough and avoid the sand traps. That takes three things: a correct understanding of what it means to be spiritual, a clear and present sense of what it means to be successful, and a plan to get you to your destination. As in golf, this requires sound advice, a basic understanding of the game, and a whole lot of practice.

WHAT DOES *SPIRITUAL* MEAN?

The title of this book contains words that are loaded with meaning—and the potential for misinterpretation. So let me be clear about my intent. The word *spiritual* is used loosely in our culture. Usually we apply it to anything that is not physical. A football running back sprints wide right out of the backfield. A linebacker comes up to meet him, puts a thunderous hit on him that you could hear in the nosebleed section of the stands, and the crowd goes wild. The play-by-play announcer says, "Wow. What a hit!" And the color guy mindlessly chimes in, "Well, you expect that kind of intensity from him. He's the spiritual leader of this team." What did he mean by that?

Or you might overhear concertgoers leaving a particularly moving symphony. One friend gushes to the other, "What a performance! That was a truly spiritual experience." Was it truly spiritual?

People today have a renewed interest in spirituality. Check out the dozens of Internet web sites devoted to spirituality, or scan the bulletin board at your local café or grocery store. People by the thousands are attending seminars, practicing yoga, hanging crystals around the house, burning incense—doing all kinds of things to get in touch with their spiritual side. They're into meditation, sensory deprivation, therapeutic touch, psychic hotlines and more, all in an attempt to achieve a higher degree of spirituality.

Because of the widespread confusion about spirituality, let me state this plainly: In this book, I mean spiritual in the sense that our success is empowered by the presence and power of the Holy Spirit.

We can try to get in touch with our spiritual side and still come up dry. But it is the Spirit's power, not human effort, that makes us successful in spiritual things. Indeed, whatever is done in our own power is profoundly unsuccessful in eternal terms. When instructing the prophet Zechariah about the nature of true success, God said, "'Not by might nor by power, but by My Spirit,' says the LORD of hosts" (Zechariah 4:6).

After Jesus' resurrection, on that first Pentecost, He promised His disciples, "But you shall receive power when the Holy Spirit has come upon you" (Acts 1:8). That's Spirit power. All the influence and effectiveness of the first-century church can be boiled down to this: Its success was not magical, numerical, managerial, or personal; its success was spiritual—Holy Spiritual. Those early Christians accomplished what was eternally meaningful only to the extent that it was accomplished through them by God's Spirit.

In that regard, nothing has changed in the intervening millennia. Any success you or I have on our spiritual journey will be accomplished by the power of the resurrected Christ living through us.

WHAT DOES SUCCESS MEAN?

Like spirituality, *success* is a word we hear frequently in our society. Most people will tell you that success means achieving your goals. It means winning. It means developing a solid, well-rounded financial portfolio. It means climbing to the top of your profession. It means meeting the perfect man or woman. It means finishing your Ph.D. and graduating with honors. It means acquiring all the trappings of prosperity—a nice house, a fancy car, a snazzy wardrobe.

Success is what everybody is after, whether in sports, business, education, or love. We all want to be successful, to achieve a favorable outcome to whatever we set our minds to. So to be spiritually successful must mean to come in first in spiritual living, right? Hardly.

The biblical concept of success in our English Bible translations comes from the Hebrew word *sakal*, which means so much more than coming in first or hitting your goal. It means to be prudent, to wisely understand, or to prosper.

At his death, King David charged his son Solomon to walk in God's ways, keep His statutes and His commandments, His judgments, and His testimonies, "that you may prosper *[sakal]* in all that you do" (1 Kings 2:3). In biblical terms, success has as much to do with behaving wisely as it does with prospering materially. First Samuel 18:5 says, "So David went out wherever Saul sent him, and behaved wisely *[sakal]*." Success, according to the Bible's definition, is a way of life, not just the attainment of a one-time goal. As the psalmist wrote, "I will behave wisely *[sakal]* in a perfect way.... I will walk within my house with a perfect heart" (101:2).

Spiritual success is learning how to live in such a way as to prosper in godly things. It means learning to live so you achieve God's "well done" at the end of your life. Notice I said, "learning to live." After all, success has to be *learned* before it can be *achieved*. You and I can learn how to be successful, but to be spiritually successful we have to learn the right things—spiritual things.

HOW I LEARNED THE SECRETS

At the time of this writing, I have just celebrated my fiftieth birthday. Those who know me will say, "Wait a minute. You're older than fifty." Well, that's true. I was born in 1944, so in terms of calendar years, fifty went whizzing by some time ago. But I have recently celebrated my fiftieth spiritual birthday. That March night by the old potbellied stove was fifty years ago. In more than half a century of walking with the Lord, I've learned some things about how to be successful and enjoy the spiritual journey at the same time. I've included those secrets in this book.

Some of the spiritual secrets were passed on to me by my spiritual mentors. These were my faithful Sunday school teachers when I was a boy, people who wondered, *Is this kid ever going to get it?* They did their job well. I got it, finally. Some of my mentors were college professors. They poured their lives into me. They were largely unsung heroes. But their advice and example "took," and I am a product of their wise counsel and diligent teaching.

Surely my father and mother were my chief mentors in the secrets to spiritual success. My father, a faithful pastor, was a simple, easy-to-understand preacher. Sermon preparation was a struggle for him, but the way he worked and lived for the Lord had a much more profound effect on me than did his preaching. He taught me to work hard, and more important, he *showed* me how to work hard. And my mother...is there any Bible story that woman doesn't know? She taught my two brothers and me everything she knew about the Bible. And she did the same for my children. I'll never forget the time decades ago when I walked into my parents' house and found my mother sprawled out on the blue carpet with my young children gathered around her in amazement. When I asked what they were doing, Mom said, "We're learning the story of Jonah and the whale." The kids each took a turn playing Jonah, the blue carpet served as the sea, and (of course) Grandma was the whale. On my spiritual journey—and my kids'—the secrets to spiritual success were taught and modeled by my parents.

Some of the secrets contained in this book were learned the hard way through years of personal struggle. God's ways were frequently not my ways. Sometimes He didn't make sense to me. I know I didn't make sense to Him. I remember a time early in my ministry when I was so discouraged with my lack of spiritual progress that I used to sit silently in the dark, listening to music on Christian radio, asking God to help me overcome my stubborn pride and obstinance. I have struggled just as you have. The Christian life often seems to be a series of alternating sprints and stumbles. But what I've learned through my struggles is that there are reasons why we are or are not spiritually successful.

Most of the secrets included in this book I have gleaned from the "Manual for Spiritual Success" that we all possess—God's Word. Years ago, I discovered a simple yet amazing principle: The more I read and grasped the guidelines set down in the Bible, and the more I dedicated myself to follow them, the more spiritual success I enjoyed. The more of it I read, the more I believed. The more I believed, the more I put into practice. The more I put into practice, the more successful my spiritual journey became. There was a cause-and-effect relationship. Does this sound obvious? Of course it is! Nevertheless, far too many Christians fail to see (or act upon) the link between biblical input and effective life output.

The Bible is not a dry book of history; it is a repository of secrets for spiritual success. As God told Joshua, "This Book of the Law shall not depart from your mouth, but you shall meditate in it day and night, that you may observe to do according to all that is written in it. For then you will make your way prosperous, and then you will have good success" (Joshua 1:8). You can be just as successful on your spiritual journey as Joshua was on his. After all, you have the same God, the same Bible, the same potential.

A PLAN FOR THE DESTINATION

During the summer of 1984, with my wife, Linda, and our four children—Tracy, Tim, Tina, and Tiffany—we set out in our van from our home in upstate New York toward the West Coast. At the time, I was president of Practical Bible College, and this trip was designed to canvass the alumni banquet circuit and be a family vacation at the same time. That summer we visited more than forty states in six weeks.

We drove west along the northern route, stopping at Mt. Rushmore, Yellowstone National Park, and a rodeo in Cody, Wyoming, on our way to the great Northwest. From there we drove down the coast of California all the way to Tijuana, Mexico. Some days we made great progress; other days our progress was slow. But along the way, we saw a gun fight in Dodge City, rode to the top of the Arch in St. Louis, and even got an autograph from the legendary football coach Bear Bryant in Tuscaloosa. Before we returned home, we had seen much of the United States from ground level.

There is no way that trip would have happened without a wonderful family, willing to put up with extreme heat (the van's AC didn't work) and countless hours of listening to Andy Williams croon on the stereo (my children still remind me about that). It also wouldn't have happened without a plan. We charted a course and stuck to it.

As with long road trips, our spiritual journey requires a plan, a strategy, if it is going to be successful. That's what this book does—it helps you chart a course for your spiritual life.

Naturally, we'll begin at the beginning. There can be no spiritual journey without a personal encounter with Jesus Christ. We'll check our vital signs. We want to know for sure that we are alive because corpses don't travel well. Just as an EMT checks for vital signs on a victim when he or she arrives at the scene of an accident, so we must make sure the evidences of new birth are present in our life. If our vitals are good, we can proceed to the next secret to spiritual growth.

Chasing spiritual success will be like chasing windmills if we don't develop a thirst for God, a thirst that is unquenchable apart from Him. Intimacy requires time, focus, and commitment. God deserves all of these from us. But more than that, our success in spiritual things will be in direct proportion to our desire for God, and that's something we have to develop as soon as we are spiritually alive.

Next, we need to develop good growth habits. When a baby is born, the mother feeds him milk and later baby food. But if a baby is to grow into an adult, he must learn to eat adult food and to feed himself. Spiritual growth relies on the same process, developing and using good habits of diet and exercise. We'll see what those habits are and find ways to improve them.

If we truly want to be successful, we will not be afraid to enlist superior help on our journey. People do that all the time. Football teams have strength and conditioning coaches. Some individuals have personal trainers. Students frequently make use of gifted tutors. Spiritual success requires help just as much as any other endeavor does. Fortunately, God has already provided superior help for us. The Holy Spirit is God's gift to us to help us grow and mature in our Christian life. What's more, God provides friends, mentors, and seasoned veterans of the faith to encourage us and challenge us. Help is available—we just need to find it and tap into it.

Next in our plan for spiritual success is to learn how to manage temptation. Nothing slows our journey from spiritual infancy to spiritual maturity as effectively as temptation. Temptation is Satan's way of getting us to take a detour on our journey toward heaven. Sometimes he puts roadblocks in our way, but more often he get us to take the scenic yet distracting route. Such temptations can be managed, and the Bible gives significant insight into temptation-control techniques.

Let's face it; sometimes we do take those side roads into sin. Try as we might to be successful, we often stumble and fall. When we do, we must not stay down. We have to get up, brush ourselves off, take a look at the map, and start out on our journey again. We must know how to quickly regain the momentum. If we don't, we will become one more name in a long list of spiritual "also rans."

Finally, if we are to reach our destination, we have to keep our eye on the goal. Every day when my family and I were on our cross-country trip, we checked the map to see where we were in relation to home. The journey was exciting; we enjoyed the things we saw along the way. But after being on the road a while, the goal was to get back home. For Christians to achieve success, we have to look beyond the grave to the glory, beyond the cross to the crown, beyond the race to the reward.

To solidify these secrets in your mind and life, you'll find a "success survey" at the end of each chapter. These surveys present questions to help you assess your spiritual progress. They may be difficult questions, but answering honestly will give you a clear vision of where you are on your journey.

STRUGGLING TOWARD SUCCESS

Our society is filled with countless schemes for finding success in every imaginable way. We are bombarded with advertisements for easy ways to get rich, get slim, get younger looking, get promoted, get respect, or get loved. Thumbing through a magazine in my doctor's office recently, I smiled at the variety of advertisements and their fantastic claims. One headline read: "The Secret to Losing Weight When You're Over 40." The copy line below said, "When you hit 40, there's an amazing little secret that makes losing weight—and keeping it off—easy." Another ad said, "No Time to Work Out?" and offered an electronic workout muscle exerciser. No more going to the gym. This device was equal to four hundred sit-ups a day (who does four hundred sit-ups anyway?). The price was only $199.95. Have you seen the "Work at Home" ads promising that you can make "up to" forty thousand dollars a year? It all sounds too simple, doesn't it? If it sounds too good to be true, it probably is.

Obviously, success in the Christian life cannot be reduced to just doing seven things. That's much too simplistic. Christian living is a lot more complicated than that. The journey is too challenging for a list of "do this" and "do that." That's why you need to be familiar with the whole Bible, not just bits and pieces of it. And that's why you need the Holy Spirit to be your encourager and your helper (see John 14:26). There is no spiritual success without yielding your life to the Spirit. Moreover, the Christian life is a personal relationship with the Creator, and no relationship can be reduced to a rote formula or one-size-fits-all program. God meets you and matures you in unique ways.

Having said that, I think you will agree that success arises from doing the right things. Whether it's a political campaign, a trip, or a golf game, following certain principles and practices tends to lead to success. There may not be any quick fix, surefire formulas for mastering the Christian life, but we can adopt healthy habits that will immeasurably enhance our potential for success. That is the spirit in which I present the seven secrets in this book.

I pray that you will not only benefit from reading 7 Secrets to Spiritual Success, but that you will struggle in the process. Does that sound strange? Well, nothing worth achieving is ever achieved easily. Spiritual success is worth the struggle.

In 1982, Kerri Strug of Tucson, Arizona, decided she wanted to be a gymnast. Since that time, she has been a great one. Kerri has been a member of five World Championship teams since 1991. She was a 1992 Olympic bronze medalist and three-time World Championship medalist. But who will ever forget her heroic efforts at the 1996 Olympics? The four-foot-eight-inch dynamo charged down the runway, vaulted through the air, and landed on an ankle already so badly sprained that it could hold her upright only for a second. It was just long enough, however, to ensure the first gold medal ever won by a U.S. Women's Gymnastics Team. The crowd of over thirty-two thousand cheered as the diminutive gymnast struggled toward success. Success is always sweeter when it is won through extraordinary efforts.

Be successful. God has given you the manual; He has given you a divine Helper; He has given you a pattern in the Savior. I pray that in the pages that follow, you will come to embrace the seven secrets to spiritual success that have helped me and so many others of your fellow strugglers. You already possess all the ingredients you need to be a spiritual success.

CHECK FOR VITAL SIGNS

I'd rather know a few things for certain than to be sure
of a lot of things that aren't so.
JOSH BILLINGS

We know that we have passed from death to life.
1 JOHN 3:14

—◦◦◦—

I have always said, with tongue in cheek, that the second happiest day of your life is the day you bring that first little baby home from the hospital. Your life is filled with joy you didn't know existed. But the happiest day of your life is the day you marry off your last child. Suddenly you discover someone you've neglected for a quarter of a century—your spouse.

Although Linda and I cherished the opportunity to raise each of our children, we have enjoyed our empty nest. We have rediscovered each other since our children have grown and gone. When all your kids are married and your responsibility to them is decreased, you also discover something else you never had—a little extra cash.

It's surprising how much money is freed up when you no longer have teenagers to feed. Your telephone bill shrivels like a pickle in a microwave. Mountains of laundry dwindle to a single basket. Soccer matches still take place on Saturday, but instead of sitting in a lawn chair on the sidelines, now you sit in your easy chair at home. And the greatest thing: With no children in the home, you realize there are dozens of restaurants that don't have golden arches in front of them. Ah, the freedom of the empty nest!

We love ethnic food. You name it—Chinese, Indian, Moroccan, French, Arabic, German—if it has a taste and aroma all its own, count us in. Soon after our last daughter was married, we happened upon a little Mexican place called La Paloma. It's just a "greasy spoon" joint, but we enjoy going there. There's not

23

a booster chair in the whole place. Judging from the clientele, it seems others our age have discovered it, too.

In the front, right by a big window, is a corner booth where we sometimes sit. A half dozen plants and a cactus are permanent fixtures in the window. The plants seem to be doing well. Their stems are green and healthy. Their flowers bloom brightly. They seem to enjoy the smell of habernos sauce in the air. The cactus is a different story. It's spiny branches have become hollow and dry. They droop over the edge of the pot like hair soaked too long in conditioner. The cactus is not green and growing. In fact, it is a sickly brown. No sign of life exists at all, and for a good reason. The cactus is dead, deceased, exterminated, expired. Never mind that the waitress told me it's looking much better lately. That cactus is dead. I'm no plant doctor, but I'd be willing to bet there are no vital signs.

SIGNS OF LIFE

Checking for vital signs is common in many professions today. Botanists do it when they have successfully produced a hybrid hibiscus. They "baby" their darling new flower, looking for any sign of stress. Auto mechanics check a car's diagnostics to determine what's wrong. Nurses in intensive care units keep close tabs on their patients by checking heart monitors. When EMTs arrive on the scene of an accident, the first thing they do is check for a pulse. Even pilots do a preflight check of their airplane before they take off. They call it a "walk around."

I asked my neighbor, who is a United Airlines pilot, what he looks for during a walk around.

"You name it," he replied. "Anything from dents in the nose cone to leaks in the hydraulic fluid. We read gauges in the wheel well, check fire extinguishers for pressure, and make sure nothing is in the engine intake." (He once found a Coke can in the engine intake of his plane, left there by a careless mechanic.) In short, pilots get a "read" on the general condition of the plane.

You can do the same thing with your spiritual life. If you have been born again, there should be signs of that new birth. If you have found new life in Christ, there should be evidence. Examining your life for signs of spiritual vitality is like skinning the bark off a branch. The outside may look a bit crusty and old, but strip a piece of that branch with your penknife, and underneath you will see bright and beautiful green. That's the sign of life in a branch; that's a vital sign. If there are no real signs of life in your Christian experience, there is likely no *experience* either.

It's no secret that you can't be spiritually successful if you aren't a Christian. You need new life, and the Bible is clear that only Christ can bring that. Jesus' ability to provide life is a favorite theme of the Gospel of John. Jesus said, "For God so loved the world that He gave His only begotten Son, that whoever believes in Him should not perish but have everlasting life" (3:16). Jesus presented Himself to the world as "the bread of life" (6:48), the giver of abundant life (10:10), "the resurrection and the life" (11:25), and "the way, the truth, and the life" (14:6).

John the Baptist agreed, saying, "He who believes in the Son has everlasting life" (3:36). And when some disciples deserted Jesus, He turned to the Twelve and asked, "Do you also want to go away?" Peter piped up and said, "Lord, to whom shall we go? You have the words of eternal life. Also we have come to believe and know that You are the Christ, the Son of the living God" (6:67–69). Having evidence of this kind of life, new life in Christ, is the very basis for spiritual success.

So what should you look for? If you are taking your pulse or doing a walk around to see if there really is evidence of salvation in your life, what are the vital signs you should spot? Here are a few of the signs that will tell you if you're spiritually alive.

LOOK FOR EVIDENCE OF FAITH

Whether we realize it or not, all of life is a walk of faith. We put our faith in many things and many people, sometimes foolishly. How do you know that the next burger you eat at your favorite fast-food place will not contain contaminated beef and make you sick? You don't; you wolf it down by faith. How do you know that the person speeding toward you on the highway doesn't have a blood alcohol level two times higher than the legal limit? You don't; you drive by faith. How do you know the pilot of your plane is competent to fly that complex piece of machinery? You don't; you fly by faith. Most of life is lived with little thought as to how much faith we have in others.

It's like that when you are saved. You come to believe that you are a sinner, because the Bible says so (Romans 3:10, 23; Psalm 51:5). You know you can't save yourself, because the Bible says so (Isaiah 64:6; Luke 18:26–27). You believe only Jesus Christ can save you from your sins—again, because the Bible says so (Acts 4:12; Luke 19:10). But can you trust what the Bible says? What if the Bible is not the Word of God as it claims to be (2 Timothy 3:16)? What if it is just a collection of fairy tales as some of your friends insist? What if your grandmother and grandfather were just naive to believe the Bible? What then?

The Book you can trust

One of the vital signs that indicates you are alive in Christ is that you believe God's promises recorded in the Bible are actually going to happen. Everybody must trust something, and Christians trust the Bible. Christians no longer see the Bible as a family heirloom or an ancient relic; they accept it for what it claims to be—the revelation of the mind of God to the minds of men (2 Peter 1:21). You see evidences of faith in what God told you, and you take those evidences of faith as strong indicators that you really are saved.

Regardless of how you viewed the Bible in the past, and despite the fact that you don't understand everything you read now, you begin to think that maybe your grandparents (or childhood Sunday school teacher or churchgoing neighbor) had something modern technocrats and skeptics do not have—an evidence of faith in God and the promises of His Word.

Do you find yourself more open to what God says in His Word than ever before? Do you get your Bible out and read it more often? Do you look for answers in its pages, anticipating that you will find them? Do you find yourself trusting the promises of God? Well, don't look now, but those are vital signs of true faith.

Confidence in promises

The apostle Paul said, "For I am persuaded that neither death nor life, nor angels nor principalities nor powers, nor things present nor things to come, nor height nor depth, nor any other created thing, shall be able to separate us from the love of God which is in Christ Jesus our Lord" (Romans 8:38–39). Do you agree? Are you gaining in the kind of confidence Paul had that nothing can separate you from God's love? That's a vital sign.

Do you believe it when you read Jesus' words in John 10:28: "I give them eternal life, and they shall never perish; neither shall anyone snatch them out of My hand"? When you wholeheartedly affirm the promises of Jesus, that's a vital sign. It's like finding the green beneath the bark. It means there's life.

Do you want to jump up and shout "Amen!" when you hear confident statements of faith like Paul's: "For I know whom I have believed and am persuaded that He is able to keep what I have committed to Him until that Day" (2 Timothy 1:12)? When you find yourself believing what you previously doubted about God and His Word, you are staring a vital sign right in the face.

LOOK FOR EVIDENCE OF HOPE

Is there any commodity in shorter supply these days than hope? Dante wrote over the entrance to hell in his *Inferno,* "Abandon hope, all who enter here." But you don't have to go all the way to the gates of hell to find hopelessness. Pick up the newspaper. Read the stories of random violence in our high schools. Students who exhibited no signs of violent behavior show up at school one day with guns and shoot a dozen students and some teachers. Their hopelessness drove them to despair.

Check the exit polls from the last election. People feel hopeless about our political system and elected officials. Oh sure, every now and then you meet a bright and cheery person who is filled with hope, but most wonder if these people really understand the gravity of the situation. The national debt continues to hang over our heads like Damocles' sword. Scandals arise in political circles, dampening our hopes of ever finding a leader who won't look us in the eye and lie to our face.

The suicide rate is higher than ever. Teenage drug use continues to skyrocket. Divorce has reached epidemic proportions.

Is there any hope?

Maybe your thoughts have been dominated by pessimism. But now that you have trusted Christ as Savior, are you beginning to see a glimmer of hope? Do you have hope that one day Christ will take you out of this mess to live with Him forever (John 14:1–3)? Are you finding renewed hope in the future because you have a renewed future yourself? Paul told Titus that the reason we have been justified by God's grace is that "we should become heirs according to the hope of eternal life" (Titus 3:7). As a result of being drawn to Jesus Christ in salvation, are you beginning to experience a personal hope of eternal life? That's a vital sign.

The apostle Peter said, "Blessed be the God and Father of our Lord Jesus Christ, who according to His abundant mercy has begotten us again to a living hope through the resurrection of Jesus Christ from the dead, to an inheritance incorruptible and undefiled and that does not fade away, reserved in heaven for you" (1 Peter 1:3–4). One proof that new birth is present in our life is hope— hope that is alive and growing as we grow in our Christian life.

If you have more hope today about the future than you did before you became a Christian, that's a vital sign. The new birth is "into a living hope," and when you are truly saved you will see some evidences of this hope, a hope that brings you happiness (Psalm 146:5) and blessing (Jeremiah 17:7); a "hope of eternal life which God, who cannot lie, promised before time began" (Titus 1:2). If you are trusting God, you are hoping in God, and that's when you begin to know you are saved.

LOOK FOR EVIDENCE OF LOVE

One of the most vital of vital signs for a Christian is the presence of love. When we are saved, for the first time we truly find ourselves loving God, not for what He can do for us but just because He is God. Before we were saved, He was God—the Just, the Holy, the One who seemed to be displeased at all the things we liked to do. But now that we have a new and dynamic relationship with Him, we see Him as our loving, gentle Father.

When asked what was the greatest commandment of the Law, Jesus replied, "'You shall love the LORD your God with all your heart, with all your soul, and with all your mind.' This is the first and great commandment" (Matthew 22:37–38). Think about it. Before you were saved, you didn't have a clue how the Christians you knew could love God so much, and now it's all so clear. God is love, He is loving, and He is lovable.

Tough to love

Just as Christians have a love for God, they also have a new kind of love for other people. It's not a perfect love, and it may not be on a par with those saintly people who have walked with the Lord for decades, but it's definitely love, and it's definitely different from what it used to be.

Bob and Edna didn't see much to like in their neighbor, Harv. A cigar-smoking truck driver, he was seldom home to keep his lawn and yard trimmed. Consequently, it looked about as ragged as his unkempt hair. His dog barked at Bob and Edna and their children whenever any of them ventured into their yard, and on more than one occasion the dog had wreaked havoc with the garbage when they set it out for collection. When they tried gently talking with him about the dog, Harv seemed to blow off their complaints—"He's a good dog. He don't hurt nobody. I keep him fenced in." Harv ignored the fact that the mongrel was a skilled digger for whom a fence was no barrier.

"I'd like to make friends with Harv," Bob told Edna one day, "but all the griping, the constant cigar smoke, and that dog—I just don't know."

Loving God is not so hard. But what about the Harvs of your life? What about that guy in the apartment above you who plays his music so loud that the glasses shake in your kitchen cupboard and the pictures rattle on the wall. What about him? Jesus no sooner said that loving God was the greatest commandment when He had the audacity to continue, "And the second is like it: 'You shall love your neighbor as yourself'" (Matthew 22:39).

I know your objections (I've had difficult neighbors, too). That guy is selfish, loud, offensive, and disagreeable. Does becoming a believer automatically make it easy for you to love him? Probably not, but the very fact that you are concerned about loving him should tell you God has done a work in your heart. Before you were saved, loving your neighbor wasn't even on your "to do" list. Evidence of love, or at least the desire to love, is a vital sign. Growing in grace will turn that desire into action.

Love in the strawberry patch

I remember when my parents demonstrated this lesson for me. I was ten years old at the time, and our family had planted two acres of strawberries on the back field of our farm. As you may know, strawberry plants do not bear fruit the first year, and they take a lot of care after that.

By the third year, when our strawberries were producing wonderfully, well, our neighbor came out one evening while we were working the patch and said,

"I had the surveyors here, and they've determined that ten feet of your strawberry patch is on my property. I'm here to pick my berries."

We had worked those strawberries for three years, weeded the patch, carefully replaced the runners back into the rows, and now we were ready to enjoy the fruit of our labors. Our neighbor had done nothing; still he came to pick our berries, and he had the nerve to do so right before our eyes.

My parents never complained. They treated this fellow cordially, never showing him anything but Christ's love. He needed the Savior, and that was foremost in their minds. That's the way Christians express their love.

Love as evidence of life

It's legitimate to ask, "Do you mean that my love for people, even nasty people, is a proof of my salvation?" Consider this: "We know that we have passed from death to life, because we love the brethren. He who does not love his brother abides in death" (1 John 3:14). Can't argue with that. And this: "God is love, and he who abides in love abides in God, and God in him" (1 John 4:16). Do you want proof that God lives in you? Think back to before you were saved. Do you see any more love in yourself now than you did then? If so, God's Word says that's evidence of salvation.

Your life of love may not be perfect yet; it may not be totally sincere love (Romans 12:9; 2 Corinthians 6:6), totally forgiving love (Ephesians 4:2), or totally honest love (Ephesians 4:15), but it is growing (Philippians 1:9; 1 Thessalonians 3:12), and that's a good sign, a vital sign.

LOOK FOR EVIDENCE OF JOY

When C. S. Lewis wrote his spiritual autobiography, he entitled it *Surprised by Joy*. Lewis was an English intellectual, a professor at Oxford, and an agnostic. For years he resisted the sweet wooing of the Holy Spirit. For years he was miserable. Then he gave in to God and, in his words, was "brought in kicking, struggling, resentful, and darting his eyes in every direction for a chance of escape."[1]

In his stubborn English intellectual pride, Lewis was not seeking a dynamic relationship with God. But when he encountered the living Christ in a saving way, Lewis's life was changed immediately, dramatically, permanently. For the first time in his life, he knew what it was to have real joy.

Unparalleled joy

Joy is quite different from other emotions. Often people confuse joy with pleasure. Sometimes they confuse joy with happiness. But joy is the unique possession of those who have had their sins forgiven and are on their way to heaven.

In the first chapter of his first letter to God's scattered people, the apostle

Peter reminded those believers that they had a living hope and an inheritance that could never spoil or fade. He also said they weren't home in heaven yet, and they would face difficult trials before they got there. The apostle knew they needed some encouragement; they needed to be assured of Jesus' love and care for them at that moment, not just when they would see Him face to face. Here are Peter's words of encouragement: "Though now you do not see Him, yet believing, you rejoice with joy inexpressible and full of glory, receiving the end of your faith—the salvation of your souls" (1 Peter 1:8–9).

Their goal—a home in heaven with Jesus forever—had not yet been achieved, but it was certain. How could they know? Because at that very moment, even with the hardships they had to endure, those Christians were filled with an inexpressible and glorious joy. Hardships may diminish joy, but they can never extinguish it.

Unexplainable joy

When speaking of the churches of Macedonia, Paul juxtaposed "a great trial of affliction" and "deep poverty" with "the abundance of joy" (2 Corinthians 8:1–2). To the world, this concept doesn't make much sense, but then again the world has never experienced the joy of salvation.

When you place your faith in Jesus as Savior, a new emotion wells up within you that you never knew existed. It is joy. It's joy that comes both by the aid of, and as proof of, the presence of the Holy Spirit in your life (Acts 13:52; Romans 15:13; 1 Thessalonians 1:6). Jesus provides for that joy in His atonement (Romans. 5:11), and everyone who looks to Him for salvation experiences it.

Admittedly, sometimes we don't feel that joy as strongly as we should. David's sin with Bathsheba robbed him of the presence of this joy. But in Psalm 51:10–12, he cried out to God in confession, "Create in me a clean heart, O God, and renew a steadfast spirit within me. Do not cast me away from Your presence, and do not take Your Holy Spirit from me. Restore to me the joy of Your salvation." Like hardships, sin can tarnish our joy, but knowledge of our salvation keeps it alive.

Inexpressible joy

Read what the apostle Jude expressed in the beautiful doxology ending his tiny epistle: "Now to Him who is able to keep you from stumbling, and to present you faultless before the presence of His glory with exceeding joy, to God our Savior, Who alone is wise, be glory and majesty, dominion and power, both now and forever" (24–25). You can't help but be impressed with the strong elements of this doxology:

Security—"able to keep you from stumbling"
Purpose—"to present you faultless before the presence of His glory"

Emotion—"with exceeding joy"

Duration—"both now and forever"

It's difficult to describe the feeling of joy—Peter did say it was "inexpressible and full of glory." But when Jesus Christ enters your life, you have a sense of peace and joy you never had before, and those around you who are not born again do not have now. The surprising thing about salvation is not the feeling of relief that your sins are forgiven, but the feeling of joy that you are secure in Christ forever. "Let all those rejoice who put their trust in You; let them ever shout for joy" (Psalm 5:11).

LOOK FOR EVIDENCE OF OBEDIENCE

Faith is intangible. Hope is intangible. Love is intangible. These are the big three (as 1 Corinthians 13:13 says, "And now abide faith, hope, love, these three; but the greatest of these is love"). Like joy, these three attributes are hard to get your hands around. If you want evidence that you are really saved, emotions are not always the best place to look. But there is one piece of hard evidence, the kind that is admissible in a court of law. Tangible evidence. Material evidence. Discernible evidence. It's obedience.

We don't always place a premium on obedience. King Saul learned the hard way that "to obey is better than sacrifice" (1 Samuel 15:22). But God considers obedience to be extremely important. In fact, so important is this quality to God that His Word says simple obedience is one of the best hard evidence proofs of salvation.

The desire to obey

How do we be assured that we know God, that our salvation is genuine? The answer is provided in 1 John 2:3: "Now by this we know that we know Him, if we keep His commandments." When we know God, we want to do what He says. That doesn't mean we *always* will do what He says, and it doesn't mean we have a new desire to obey Christ whereas before we had none at all.

John repeats two verses later: "But whoever keeps His word, truly the love of God is perfected in him. By this we know that we are in Him" (1 John 2:5). There it is in black and white. If you believe God and His Word, you have to believe this. You have no other choice. The proof of salvation is obedience, not *perfect* obedience (or else none of us would be saved), but a *desire* for obedience.

Years ago in a tiny village, there was a mean man who sold wood to his neighbors. He always took advantage of them by cutting his logs a few inches under the required four feet. One day the miserly man came to trust Jesus Christ as Savior, and word spread through the village like wildfire. Nobody believed what they heard; they all thought this man was beyond God's reach. But soon a man came running into the grocery store and shouted, "It's true. He has become a Christian."

When asked how he knew it was true, the man said, "I went over to his house and measured the wood he cut yesterday. It was a good four feet long."

That's the way it is. Salvation brings a desire for obedience.

What's more, obedience has a way of gaining momentum. One form of obedience always leads to another. As Oswald Chambers observed:

> Obey God in the thing He shows you, and instantly the next thing is opened up. One reads tomes on the work of the Holy Spirit, when five minutes of drastic obedience would make things as clear as a sunbeam. "I suppose I shall understand these things someday!" You can understand them now. It is not study that does it, but obedience.
>
> The tiniest fragment of obedience, and heaven opens and the profoundest truths of God are yours straight away. God will never reveal more truth about Himself until you have obeyed what you know already.[2]

If you really want to know if you're saved, look for obedience to the Savior. It's tangible proof.

LOOK FOR EVIDENCE OF FRUIT

A friend of mine named Philip lives in Florida and used to own a number of orange groves. Sitting in his living room one evening awaiting dinner, we chatted about orange trees—how long they bear fruit, why some produce more than others, how to keep them from freezing. It was then that Philip shared his theory about bearing fruit.

"Have you noticed that every living thing has a desire to reproduce itself?" he said. "No plant or animal wants to leave this earth without bearing offspring, and it seems that the closer a tree or a person is to death, the stronger the instinct to reproduce becomes."

With tongue in cheek, Philip said this is why nurses in hospitals have to watch out for the little old men. "When these old guys with their spindly legs and toothless mouths think they are about to expire," he said, "they get the strangest urge to flirt with the nurses. They have a stronger impulse to reproduce than they have had in years."

To further argue his point, Philip gave me an example from his orange groves. "Evidence of life, even if there is little outward evidence, can be found when a tree shows signs that it wants to bear fruit," he said. When this veteran orange grower had an old orange tree that was producing less fruit than the others, he would take an ax and chop around the roots of the tree rather than cut it down.

"The tree thought that was the end for it, and the next year it would produce more than the others," Philip said with a laugh.

The moral of this story is simple: Where there is life, there is the desire to produce fruit. Where there is spiritual life, there is the desire to bear spiritual fruit. As Paul said, "The fruit of the Spirit is love, joy, peace, longsuffering, kindness, goodness, faithfulness, gentleness, self-control. Against such there is no law. And those who are Christ's have crucified the flesh with its passions and desires" (Galatians 5:22–24).

What did the apostle mean? If you belong to Christ Jesus, there will be a change in the kind of fruit your life bears. Before salvation there was adultery, fornication, lewdness, selfish ambitions, dissentions, and so on (vv. 19–20). After salvation there is love, joy, peace, longsuffering, kindness, and self-control (vv. 22–23). Knowing if you're saved may just be a matter of inspecting fruit.

Picking from a different tree

What do you see in your own life? Have your friends noticed a difference in your life? Do your old buddies or girlfriends keep asking, "Why don't you want to go drinking with us anymore?" Do your old friends avoid you? Little wonder. They don't have a taste for the fruit of your new life in Christ. Your new life can be an effective witnessing tool, but don't be surprised if some people don't want the kind of fruit you have to offer.

If you are saved, something different about you will be noticed by those who used to pick fruit from the tree of your life. They'll know you're different, and so will you. You may not yet be bearing the kind of fruit that more mature trees in the grove are bearing, but if the fruit is different on the outside, that means something is different on the inside.

Wayne Grudem poses the question, "What will serve as evidence of genuine conversion?" The answer, he says, rests in an honest response to three other questions:

- Do I have a present trust in Christ for salvation?
- Is there evidence of a regenerating work of the Holy Spirit in my heart?
- Do I see a long-term pattern of growth in my Christian life?[3]

The answers to these questions will indicate the presence or absence of spiritual vital signs.

LOOK FOR "THE 1 JOHN TWENTY"

If you're looking for more ways to take your spiritual pulse, consider the empirical evidence of "The 1 John Twenty." That is, the book of 1 John lists twenty specific signs to help you know that you are born again. Of course, it is possible to feign one of these signs and fool yourself into believing that you are saved. For example, there are some people who think that by obeying the Lord and attending church regularly they are born again. That may not be so. Church attendance neither saves nor proves salvation. But it would be difficult for you to feign all of the above vital signs and next to impossible to fake "The 1 John Twenty."

According to the epistle of 1 John, you know you're saved if:

1. *You walk in God's light* (1:6). It is the nature of God to be light, to search the darkness and bring hope for escape to the light. When you walk in God's light, you open your life to His scrutiny, allowing Him to search your life for sinful things hidden from everyone but Him. To walk in God's light, you have to know where to find it. If you have a Bible, you have God's light. His Word is a lamp to your feet and a light to your path (Psalm 119:105).

2. *You have fellowship with God's family* (1:7). This doesn't mean you become intimate friends with every Christian you know, but it does mean you feel enriched by time spent with spiritual family members. The word *fellowship* comes from the Greek word *koinonia,* which means "to share together with." When real Christians get together, they can't help but talk about those things families have in common.

3. *You have a keen sense of your own sinfulness* (1:8, 10). Because Christians have a relationship with a holy God, we know just how far we are from perfection. We understand and acknowledge our innate sinfulness, and we're bothered when we see immoral or immodest things. The Holy Spirit lives within us and convicts us constantly of sin. If your sin troubles you, it's a powerful sign that you are saved.

4. *You live in willful obedience to God's Word* (2:3, 5). Does this mean you keep every one of God's commands? Of course not. But the saved person chooses to live in submission to the Lord and His laws. When we fall short of the ideal, we confess our sin, obtain God's forgiveness, and redouble our efforts to obey.

5. *You no longer are enamored with what captivates the world* (2:15). This verse does not refer to God's creation, but rather the world system—our culture's destructive values and mores. The world is driven by success, accumulating money, getting ahead, outwitting your neighbor. It is saturated with sex and power and is energized by hedonism. But the Christian realizes that it profits him nothing if he gains the whole world and loses his own soul (Mark 8:36). So when you are born again, the attractions of the world lose their appeal.

6. *You do things that are right in God's eyes* (2:29). Righteousness is right living—living in a way that pleases God. When we live righteously, we live according to the moral and spiritual principles of God, as they are revealed to us in His Word. Unsaved people sometimes care about justice, but they care little about

righteousness. Fortunately, we have an example of Someone who did the things that are right in God's eyes—the Lord Jesus. As Jesus lived while He was on the earth, so we must live in imitation of Him.

7. *You eagerly anticipate the return of the Lord* (3:2). Are you so satisfied with your success and all you possess that you think little about heaven? Or can you hardly wait for Jesus to fulfill His promise to return for you (John 14:3)? Christians may enjoy the life God has provided here on earth, but they always have an eye toward heaven, anticipating the day we will go to live with our Father forever.

8. *You desire to live a life of purity* (3:3). A subsequent action accompanies our expectation of the Lord's return—we want to make sure we are ready when He comes. If you are a Christian, you will constantly make sure you are right with your Savior. You do this by purifying your life through repentance and confession.

9. *You have a growing freedom from sinful behavior* (3:6–10; 5:18). As I said earlier, the Christian life is a journey, not just a one-time event. Will you ever be able to live totally free from sin, free from impure thoughts and inappropriate actions? Not this side of heaven. Yet as you mature as a Christian, you should notice that sin's grip on your life is loosening. When 1 John 3:9 says anyone born of God does not sin, the verb is in the present tense. It means you will not continue in the old habits of sin. Once saved you do not perpetuate a sinful lifestyle.

10. *You have a genuine love for other believers* (3:14; 4:7). We won't always agree with our fellow Christians, and we may not always like the way they act, but we recognize that we share the same heavenly Father and the same eternal destiny. While we should love all people, Christians have a special love for those who also love their Savior.

11. *You demonstrate your love in word and deed* (3:18–19). Whoever said "talk is cheap" never had to pay my telephone bill. But the principle is true—words without corresponding deeds are empty and meaningless; they are cheap. If you are truly born again, you will want to *show* your love for other believers, not just talk about it. You do this by performing acts of kindness and grace, both little and big.

12. *You have the witness of your conscience* (3:21–22). Have you ever been heartsick over something you've said, someone you've hurt, or something you've done? We all have. What caused us to feel so bad? It was our conscience, that voice deep inside of us that nudges us to do right and needles us when we do wrong. All people have consciences, but Christians have consciences washed clean in the blood of the Lamb. We live in heightened awareness of right or wrong because we have a conscience illuminated by God's Word and instructed by God's Spirit.

13. *You have the indwelling presence of the Spirit* (3:24; 4:13). Even better than having a tiny voice inside telling you right from wrong, Christians have the immeasurable advantage of the Holy Spirit living within us. Romans 8:16 tells us that the Spirit affirms what our conscience tells us. And when Satan tries to convince us that we're not really saved, the Spirit reassures us of God's promise for eternal salvation.

14. *You have the ability to distinguish truth from error* (4:6). Before you were saved, you had little ability to understand God and His Word. First Corinthians 2:14 acknowledges that the unsaved man cannot receive the things of God or internalize them. Salvation changes all that. With salvation comes the ability to distinguish truth from error. As a Christian you must spend lots of time in God's Word so the Holy Spirit can teach you truth and enable you to identify error.

15. *You confess that Jesus is God the Son* (4:15). If people come to your door and claim that Jesus was an angel or a prophet or a good teacher but not God, you know one thing for sure—they are not born-again Christians. It is impos-sible to be saved and deny the deity of Christ. You may not have fully understood who Jesus is before you were saved, and you may not completely understand now, but you do believe that Jesus is, in fact, the Son of God.

16. *You believe that Jesus is the Christ* (2:22–23; 5:1). For centuries, since the great prophets of ancient Israel, every Jew has been anxiously awaiting *messiach*, the Messiah. Every Jewish mother made it her secret prayer that God would choose her to bare the Anointed One of God. The New Testament word for messiah is *christos* or Christ. Christians believe that God chose Mary to give birth to the Christ child. Simeon, a devout Jew whom God had promised would not die "before he had seen the Lord's Christ" (Luke 2:26), saw the baby Jesus and was immediately convinced he had seen the long-awaited Messiah. If you are convinced of the same—that Jesus of Nazareth is indeed the Messiah of Israel—that's another reason to believe that you are born from above.

17. *You exhibit "overcoming faith"* (5:4–5). If conditions in the world around you don't appear to be getting better, cheer up. The battle isn't over yet. Christians know how things will turn out. We've read the last chapter, and we know Jesus Christ will win the war. That's the essence of overcoming faith—it's a rock-solid belief that no matter what happens today, victory belongs to the Lord. All who are born again can claim victory because Jesus said, "Be of good cheer, I have overcome the world" (John 16:33).

18. *You believe the promise of God* (5:9–10, 12). The Bible is filled with promises—someone has estimated more than seven thousand of them. But some promises are of greater eternal weight than others. One such promise is 1 John 5:12: "He who has the Son has life; he who does not have the Son of God does not have life." John divides all humanity into two categories—the saved and the lost. If you

are saved, you have trusted the Son of God for your eternal destiny; if you are lost, you have rejected the Son of God and chosen your own eternal destiny. If you have the Son of God as your Savior, you are as certain of eternal life in heaven as if you were already there.

19. *You trust the purpose of God's Word* (5:13). The Bible is much more than a book of history. It's even more than a guide for life. The Bible is the revelation of the mind of God to the minds of men. God had a definite purpose when He revealed His mind. The apostle John said the whole world could not contain all the things that Jesus did (John 21:25), but the things that were recorded in the Bible were "written that you may believe that Jesus is the Christ, the Son of God, and that believing you may have life in His name" (John 20:31). God has no hidden agenda. If you have trusted Jesus Christ as your Savior, your heavenly Father wants you to be certain you are a Christian, and the Bible was written to give you that certainty.

20. *You have an understanding from the Son of God* (5:20). Have you noticed how much corruption and deceit there is in the world today? People will look right into the camera and lie to your face. Is there anything you can count on for sure? The Bible says there is. You can be sure that the Son of God came to this earth to give you the true understanding of the way things are. Jesus is the way to God; He is the one truth that you can trust; and He is the eternal life that God has promised you (John 14:6). That's the understanding you receive from the Son of God.

So what if you don't experience all of these vital signs? Does that mean there is no new life in you? No, because what you experience as a result of salvation is not what God uses to save you. These vital signs are *results;* they are not the basis for salvation. The Lord helps us grow and mature in different ways. Therefore, some of the vital signs may be stronger than others.

I have included an appendix, "How to Know You Are Saved," to provide a theological foundation for your salvation. Most people lack assurance of salvation for two reasons. First, they do not understand the basis of their salvation. Second, they do not appreciate the means of their salvation. If you get God's perspective on these issues, you'll have fewer problems with spiritual doubt. If you aren't sure you can trust your vital signs, trust your Bible.

IT'S TIME TO ACT

It would be a tragedy for you to place your ladder against the wall, climb higher and higher, spend years in the pursuit of happiness, and then discover, in the end, that your ladder was leaning against the wrong wall. If you are to be a spiritual success, you must make sure your ladder is in the right place.

Many people are trying to climb to spiritual success with their ladder leaning against their sense of morality, their church, their good works, but they are going nowhere because they are not even born again. The first and most essential secret to spiritual success is to make sure you're in God's family. Everything else in this book, every secret we consider, is of no value at all if your ladder is leaning against the wrong wall.

I want to conclude this chapter with a story that illustrates the importance of trusting Jesus alone as Savior. Years ago there was a wealthy man who, with his devoted son, shared a passion for collecting works of art. They traveled the world adding priceless Picassos, Van Goghs, Monets, and many other treasures to their family estate. The son's trained eye and sharp business mind made his father beam with pride.

One year as winter approached, war erupted, and the young man left to serve his country. A short time later, the father received a telegram notifying him that his son was killed in action. Distraught and lonely, the old man faced the upcoming holidays with anguish. On Christmas morning, the man was awakened by a knock at the door. He was greeted by a soldier who introduced himself by saying, "I was a friend of your son's. I'm the one who rescued his body when he was killed."

When the old man invited him in, the solder said, "Sir, I'm an artist, and I'd like you to have this." The old man unwrapped a package and discovered a portrait of his son. Critics and collectors would not have considered it a work of genius, but the father, overcome with grief, thanked the soldier and hung the picture above the fireplace. The painting of his son soon became his most prized possession, eclipsing any interest in the masterpieces he owned.

The following spring, the old man became ill and passed away. The art world buzzed with anticipation. Who would get the masterpieces that hung in the family gallery? According to the old man's will, all of his art would be auctioned off on Christmas Day, the day he had received his greatest gift—the portrait of his son.

The appointed day finally arrived, and the auction began with a painting that was not on any museum's list. It was the painting of the man's son. The auctioneer asked for an opening bid. The room was silent.

"Who will open the bidding at one hundred dollars?"

Minutes passed. No one spoke. From the back of the room someone shouted cynically, "Who cares about that painting? Let's go on to the great works of art."

But the auctioneer persisted, and a friend of the old man finally said, "Will you take ten dollars for the painting? That's all I have. I knew the boy, so I'd like to have it."

"I have ten dollars," called the auctioneer. "Will anyone go higher?"

After more silence, he pounded his gavel and shouted, "Going once. Going twice. Sold to the gentleman for ten dollars."

The crowd murmured but was eager to get to the real treasures. To the shock of everyone, however, the auctioneer announced that the auction was over. Stunned disbelief quieted the room.

Someone asked, "What do you mean it's over? We didn't come here for a picture of some old guy's son. What about all the other paintings—the ones that matter? There are millions of dollars of art here! I demand that you tell me what's going on."

"It's simple," the auctioneer replied. "According to the will left by the father, whoever takes the son...gets it all."

That's the way it is with eternal salvation. When you trust God's Son as your Savior, you get it all—all of God's grace, all of God's goodness, all of God's eternal delights.

Have you trusted Jesus Christ as your Savior? Was there ever a time when you realized that you were sinking in your own sin and couldn't save yourself? Did you truly believe that Jesus would save you if you sincerely asked Him? And this is important—did you ask? If the answer is yes to each of these questions, you're ready to look for vital signs and then move on to other secrets to spiritual success. If the answer is no, this is the place to begin. Going on from here without new life in Christ is like climbing a ladder that is leaning against the wrong wall.

If you and I are to achieve any measure of spiritual success, what will we have to do? Three things. We must encounter truth; we must believe it; and we must act on it.

In the Introduction, I defined spiritual success as "learning how to live in such a way as to prosper in godly things." Success, as God defines it, is vastly different from success as most people define it. Godly success is learned, primarily from God's Word, His "manual for success."

This chapter revealed the initial secret to spiritual success—knowing for sure you are born again and on your way to heaven. You have encountered the truth, do you believe it? Do you understand and believe that if you want to go to God's heaven, you have to go in God's way? Do you believe Jesus when He said, "I am the way, the truth, and the life. No one comes to the Father except through Me" (John 14:6)? That's God's honest truth and having encountered it, if you believe it, you must now act on it.

SUCCESS SURVEY #1

1. *Look deep within yourself.* Peer into the deepest reaches of your soul, the part that doesn't try to impress anybody or fool anybody. Ask yourself this question: If I were to die tonight, would I be in heaven tomorrow? And ask another, equally important question: Upon what do I base my answer? And, as long as we're looking deep and not trying to fool anybody, ask this: How sure am I of my answer?

2. *If you're not satisfied with your answers, find better ones.* If you've never trusted Jesus to be your Savior, and you feel a need to do so, turn to the Appendix and settle this issue once and for all. Will you do it right now? There is no spiritual success without Jesus.

3. *Check your spiritual vital signs.* If you know for certain that heaven is your eternal destiny, don't stop there. Move on and check for the telltale signs of spiritual growth. Can you find any evidence that the big three—faith, hope, and love—are alive and well in your life? Are you looking for that blessed hope—the glorious return of the Lord Jesus? Even if you find it tough to love a less-than-lovable neighbor, are you making progress?

4. *Determine which of "The 1 John Twenty" are present in your life.* Which are lacking? Which of these tangible evidences of salvation are you working on the hardest? Which of them have people told you they discern in your life? You may not find evidence of all twenty, but you ought to be increasing the number if you are saved and on your way to heaven.

5. *Do you know the basis for your salvation?* If someone asked you if you are a Christian, and you said yes, would you be able to explain the basis for your answer? Do you have a rock-solid foundation for your belief that you are a Christian? God has provided that foundation in His Word. If you don't have adequate reasons for why you need to have vital signs, why not check out the Appendix at the end of this book and get some answers?

DEVELOP INTIMACY WITH GOD

What this country needs is a man who knows God
other than by hearsay.
THOMAS CARLYLE

"Now set your heart and your soul to seek the LORD your God."
1 CHRONICLES 22:19

—◦◦◦—

When I was a boy, my father pastored two small churches in western Pennsylvania. He gave himself to those dear people, ministering to their needs for thirty-three years. The churches were only five miles apart, and eventually under my father's guidance, they merged and became one congregation. But when I was growing up, my family and I would attend Sunday school and morning worship at the larger of the churches, and then drive to the smaller church for Sunday school and the worship service. Get the picture? As a young boy, I attended four church services each Sunday before noon.

At the second church, there wasn't much space. It was a one-room country church with no classrooms. The leaders conquered that problem by having only three classes: The boys met in the back corner, the adults in the middle, and the girls in the opposite front corner. It seemed prudent to the ancient sages of the church to keep the boys and girls separated.

Since I had already heard the dress rehearsal of the Sunday school lesson at the other church, I often found my mind wandering during the service. One Sunday when I was seven years old, I peered across the room at the crop of young girls in the opposite corner. My eyes fell upon a seven-year-old goddess. She was wearing a gingham dress; her hair was parted in the left side, and she had a bow on the right side. My eyes sparkled like an icicle in the sun. I was in love. I mused to myself, *Maybe that's the girl I'll marry someday.* It was the kind of daydreaming that made the fourth service of the morning bearable for the preacher's kid.

Well, sometimes daydreams do come true. That little girl and I have been happily married since 1965.

Linda's family somehow drifted away from that church, and for a number of years we never saw each other. But we were reintroduced as teenagers when she began to attend the youth group of the other church my father pastored. It was with joyful gratitude that we discovered each other again.

We began dating sometime thereafter and went together for about five years before we were married. I wasn't exactly a fast mover, but I was getting to know the person I would spend the rest of my life with. Now that we have been married all these years, I continue to develop an intimacy with her that I have with no one else. It's the intimacy of our relationship that makes our lives together joyful.

As Linda and I learned during those early years together—and during all the years of our marriage—the desire to develop intimacy and closeness comes naturally when we love someone. Once we are introduced to someone we really enjoy, it's only natural to want to develop a relationship with that person. The more our love grows, the more intimate our relationship becomes.

That's the way it is in human relationships, and that's the way it should be in our relationship with God through His Son, Jesus Christ. Our love grows, and over time we want to walk with Him more and more closely.

A. W. Tozer reflected on this when he said, "To have found God and still to pursue Him is the soul's paradox of love…." St. Bernard stated this holy paradox in a musical quatrain that will be instantly understood by every worshiping soul:

We taste Thee, O Thou Living Bread,
  And long to feast upon Thee still;
We drink of Thee, the Fountainhead
  And thirst our souls from Thee to fill.[1]

If the first secret to spiritual success is to make sure you're in the family of God by checking for vital signs, the next is to allow your love for God to grow. You can be born again and get to heaven, but you can't remain a spiritual infant and reach your potential as a Christian. That takes developing intimacy with God.

WHAT IS INTIMACY WITH GOD?

The Westminster Shorter Catechism asks, "What is man's primary purpose?" The answer: "Man's primary purpose is to glorify God and to enjoy Him forever."[2] Enjoying intimacy with God is one of the choice reasons for your salvation. How is it, then, that people can muddle through their Christian lives without ever developing a close walk with God? When they live that way, they rob Him of glory and themselves of joy.

King David said, "One thing I have desired of the LORD, that will I seek: that I may dwell in the house of the LORD all the days of my life, to behold the beauty of the LORD, and to inquire in His temple" (Psalm 27:4). David wanted more than anything to have a vibrant, growing, intimate relationship with his God. He craved such a relationship.

The king did not go to the temple out of obligation or duty, as many people do today. He did not go because it was expected of him. He didn't go to get a blessing or to network with the movers and shakers of his community. He went because he thirsted after God. He wanted to gaze on the beauty of the Lord. He wanted the warmth and caring that came from an affectionate friendship with his Creator.

That's what intimacy means—warmth, caring, affection, closeness. That's what the king sought in his relationship with God, and it's what made him a spiritual giant. He was a man after God's own heart (Acts 13:22; 1 Samuel 13:14), and you can be, too!

If you want to discover the secret to spiritual success, you must crave intimacy with God the way this spiritually successful shepherd did. You cannot be happy with the superficial spirituality. You will hunger to be intimate with God the same way a bear hungers for its first meal after emerging from winter's hibernation.

DEFINING A HUNGER FOR GOD

There's an ancient tale about a young man from India who came to know Christ as his Savior. He had heard that he should hunger after God, but he wasn't exactly sure what that meant. He went for help to a wise old Christian whose close walk with the Lord was well known.

"How can I hunger after God?" the young man asked.

Without saying a word, the elderly Christian led him to a nearby river. Once there they waded into the deep water. When the river was just beneath their chins, the old Christian grabbed the younger man by the neck and pushed him under the water. He held him down until the young fellow struggled in desperation. Another minute and he would have drowned. Finally, the old man pulled his friend up out of the water and dragged him to the shore. The younger believer lay on the ground, coughing and spitting out water.

When he had sucked in sufficient air to breathe, the puzzled young man shouted, "What did you do that for? What did nearly drowning me have to do with hungering after God?"

The old man quietly replied, "While you were under the water, what did you want more than anything else?"

The young Christian thought for a minute and replied, "I wanted air. I wanted to breathe more than anything else in the world."

"When you hunger for God as much as you hungered for air, you'll find Him," the old man replied.

That's a hard lesson to learn, and nearly drowning a young believer is an extreme way to learn it, but I wonder if you feel that desperate kind of longing? Do you want to develop an intimacy with God? If so, how badly do you want that close relationship? Do you crave it the way the young Indian Christian gasped for air? Perhaps the reason so many of us have trouble being intimate with God is that we really don't want it badly enough.

As the Deer Pants

The Bible crafts a delightful image of how we are to hunger for intimacy with God. Psalm 42:1 says, "As the deer pants for the water brooks, so pants my soul for You, O God."

In your mind, transport yourself to the Promised Land, the land of this psalmist. Picture a young, reddish-brown female deer or hart, the kind that is found in the wilderness of Judea. She is alone and afraid. Her heart is racing. Her head is erect. The frightened deer's eyes dart back and forth in watchfulness. She has just bolted through the crags and ravines of the badlands that are Israel's wilderness, escaping from a dangerous predator.

This graceful animal was known for its speed and agility (Song of Solomon 8:14). It could leap high into the air as if on springs (Isaiah 35:6). So beautiful was the desert deer that the lover in the Song of Solomon likens her beloved to it (2:9). Usually such a deer would be in the company of a roe buck or male deer (Deuteronomy 12:15; 14:5; 15:22), but not this day. Today she is alone. Her nostrils flare, and her stomach heaves as she breathes heavily. She is tired and unbearably thirsty.

The Hebrew word the psalmist chose to describe this deer's longing for water is *arag*. It means to long for, cry after, or when panting, to breathe quickly, spasmodically, in a labored manner. The word is used only here and in Joel 1:20: "The beasts of the field also cry out to You, for the water brooks are dried up, and fire has devoured the open pastures." There could hardly be a better picture of extreme desire or need.

A St. Bernard in the Plains

When animals need air, they pant. Perhaps you've noticed your dog doing this. It's a natural reflex action. Linda and I have a hundred-and-fifty-pound St. Bernard named Brienz. She is a joy to have around the house (yes, she is an indoor dog; sometimes she even thinks she is a lap dog). St. Bernards were originally bred as rescue dogs in the Alps. They would travel for miles over the snow to dig out someone trapped by an avalanche. They love snow and cold weather. Unfortunately, there are no mountains in Nebraska where we live, only plains. Even so, in the dead of winter, Brienz will come to the door and beg to go out. Her favorite winter pastime is lazily lying in a pile of snow with frigid air blowing across her face.

Summer is not nearly as enjoyable for this cold-loving dog. During the hot months, Brienz is constantly on the lookout for a cool spot in the basement or on the marble entranceway by the front door. On especially hot days, you can find her lying on the floor register, sucking up the breeze from the air conditioner. Since St. Bernards "perspire" through their tongue, Brienz will slide her huge tongue out the side of her mouth and pant to allow the cool air to enter her body.

Every time I see my St. Bernard panting, I get a mental image of what the psalmist was talking about in Psalm 42:1. As Brienz pants for cold air, and as the deer pants for the refreshing mountain stream, so the Christian who knows the secret to spiritual success pants for intimacy with God.

THIRSTING AFTER GOD

The psalmist continues this striking image, adding, "My soul thirsts for God, for the living God. When shall I come and appear before God?" (42:2). This is a poetic technique to embellish the imagery and deepen our understanding of our need for God. The psalmist used the most common word for thirst in the Bible. You encounter it again and again as you read God's Word. For example, Exodus 17:3 notes that when the Israelites camped at Rephidim in the wilderness, "the people thirsted there for water." That's physical thirst, but it's the same word used here to describe our spiritual thirst.

Suppose it's a hot summer afternoon—the temperature is hovering near triple digits. You have just finished mowing the lawn when you collapse beside your spouse, who is napping in the hammock. You scowl at him or her and say, "I'm dying of thirst!" Now be honest. Were you really dying? Probably not, but you were certainly closer to death than your slumbering spouse. What you meant was you needed a drink of water so badly that you thought you'd die if you didn't get it.

That's the way it is with the Christian who has learned the second secret to spiritual success. He or she thirsts after God the same way we thirst after water when we are dehydrated. We need time with God the Father. We need fellowship with God the Son. We need closeness with God the Holy Spirit.

You can almost feel David's appetite for God as he says, "I spread out my hands to You; my soul longs for You like a thirsty land" (Psalm 143:6). It's as if he is grasping at the heavens to pull God into his intimate presence. He raises his weary hands to take hold of God. He needs to feel God's strong arms around him.

He needs closeness with God. Will he get it? Read the rest of Psalm 143 and decide for yourself.

How like the man after God's own heart are you? Do you thirst for God's power in your life? Do you thirst for His blessing? Do you need Him to show you by signs and wonders that He is still in charge? Not if you've learned the secret to spiritual success. Being a spiritual success is not craving what God can do for you. It's not thirsting for His benefits. It is thirsting for intimacy with Him.

DAVID'S EXAMPLE OF THIRST

David, as the seeker after God's heart, demonstrated his desire in Psalm 63:1: "O God, You are my God; early will I seek You; my soul thirsts for You; my flesh longs for You in a dry and thirsty land where there is no water." David's desire for intimacy is woven through this verse like the threads of a tweed jacket. They are the threads you and I need to weave these same threads into our lives if we are to develop intimacy with God. What kind of example did David give us?

First, David's thirst was for God Himself—not a hero, a feeling, or a fulfilling experience. God has revealed Himself to us, and He is completely available to us. How much of God do you want? Most people get to know only as much of God as they want to. David wasn't satisfied to know *about* God. His search for God was not mere scientific inquiry, an exercise of the mind. Nor would he be satisfied with mere emotion. David wanted substance and feeling. He was committed to seeking God earnestly. That would take a time covenant and a higher degree of commitment than most people want to allocate.

Second, David's thirst was for a personal God. He sought a relationship with a knowable and understandable God. He craved "my God," not *a* god. The shepherd king wasn't looking for a meaningful relationship with a distant deity, and neither should you. David was not interested in being intimate with the subject of Theology 101 class. He thirsted for Jehovah, the God who has a name, an identity, a personality.

Third, David's thirst for God was both physical and spiritual. David said, "My soul thirsts for you; my flesh longs for you...." The word translated *longs* is used only here in Scripture. It means to become so weak through intense longing that you will collapse if your need is not met. It's as if he is saying, "My Father, if I can't become more intimate with you, I am going to faint dead away due to weakness." David's entire being—body and soul—was set in pursuit of the Holy One.

THIRSTING FOR THE RIGHT REASON

John Piper, in his book *Desiring God*, describes himself as a "Christian hedonist." By that he means he is someone who seeks with all his heart the pleasures that come from intimacy with God. Piper says,

The pleasure Christian hedonism seeks is the pleasure which is in God himself. He is the end of our search, not the means to some further end. Our exceeding joy is he, the Lord—not the streets of gold, or the reunion with relatives or any blessing of heaven. Christian hedonism does not reduce God to a key that unlocks a treasure chest of gold and silver. Rather it seeks to transform the heart so that "the Almighty will be your gold and choice silver to you."[3]

Make certain you do not seek intimacy with God for the wrong reasons. Don't thirst for God for what you can get out of Him. Love God not what He can do for you, but because there is no equal to Him. Love God not for His benefits, but for His person.

St. Augustine spoke of his restlessness before discovering God in unforgettable words: "Thou hast have made us for Thyself, and our heart is restless, until it rest in Thee." But the restless heart is not going to be satisfied with one-time exposure to God. The restless heart will seek intimacy with the One who satisfies its deepest longing. This kind of intimacy is not found through the experience of salvation alone, but through the ongoing desire of a longing heart, thirsting after God.

THE FOUNDATION OF INTIMACY WITH GOD

Developing an intimate relationship with God is not much different from developing an intimate relationship with anyone else you love. If you meet someone who really interests you, through the course of time and by allowing your heart to guide you, you come to love that person. And while you are falling in love, you enter a meaningful and intimate relationship with that person. The same happens when we develop intimacy with God. Let's explore some aspects of God's character that will help us better understand how to develop intimacy with Him.

God seeks ever more closeness.

Realize that you can be more intimate with God than you are right now, perhaps far more intimate. Regardless of how deeply you know God, you can get to know Him better still.

On June 6, 1981, Doug Whitt and his new bride, Sylvia, were escorted to their hotel bridal suite in the wee hours of the morning. In the lovely suite the honeymooners saw a sofa, chairs, and a table—but no bed. Then they discovered that the sofa was a hide-a-bed. They opened it and climbed in. The mattress was lumpy, the springs sagging. It wasn't the night of romantic bliss they had long dreamed of. They spent their first night of married life tossing and turning, both waking in the morning with sore backs. The new husband felt they deserved so much better and his bride agreed, so he went to the hotel desk to complain.

Mildly upset, Doug explained to the desk clerk about the room. With a puzzled look on his face, the clerk queried, "Did you open the door in the room?"

"The door? Uh, no," Doug responded, "I thought it was a closet."

Returning to the room with the groom, the clerk opened the door, and there, complete with a fruit basket and chocolates, was a beautiful bridal bedroom with a lovely, big bed. It was a veritable honeymoon paradise, right behind the door that led from the living room of the suite. The couple had not ventured far enough. They had settled for too little.[4]

Often that happens with Christians who want to be successful spiritually. They settle for salvation and don't venture further to experience the joy of true intimacy with God. They think getting saved is all there is, but there is so much more. Jesus promised, "I have come that they may have life, and that they may have it more abundantly" (John 10:10).

Jonathan Edwards, best known as the preacher God used to quicken the Great Awakening in eighteenth-century America, described his own desire for a deeper intimacy with God:

> I had vehement longings of soul after God and Christ, and after more holiness, wherewith my heart seemed to be full, and ready to break.... I spent most of my time in thinking of divine things, year after year; often walking alone in the woods, and solitary places, for meditation, soliloquy, and prayer, and converse with God.... I was almost constantly in ejaculatory prayer, wherever I was. Prayer seemed to be natural to me, as the breath by which the inward burnings of my heart had vent.[5]

God initiates intimacy.

The Bible is clear that God draws us to Himself. We do not pursue God because we are superspiritual; we pursue Him because we are obedient. He draws us to Himself in salvation and then continues daily to draw us to Himself in spiritual intimacy. When we yield to His overtures, we find spiritual success.

In their popular book *Experiencing God,* Henry Blackaby and Claude King use Moses' life as an example of how we experience God. One of the authors' "Seven Realities of Experiencing God" is this: "God pursues a continuing love relationship with you that is real and personal." Blackaby and King note, "God took the initiative to come to Moses and initiate a love relationship with him that was real and personal.... Time and time again God invited Moses to talk with Him and to be with Him. God initiated and maintained a continuing relationship with Moses. This relationship was based on love, and daily God fulfilled His purposes through His 'friend' Moses."[6]

Check it out for yourself. Think of all the times in the Bible when a person's relationship with God was initiated by Him. When Adam and Eve sinned in the Garden of Eden, who pursued them to restore a lost love relationship (Genesis 3:8–9)? Did Noah come to God in the midst of his wicked world, or did God go to Noah (Genesis 6:11–13)? God came to Abraham (Genesis 12:1–3). He came to each of the prophets (1 Samuel 3:1–11). Jesus came to Peter and the disciples (Matthew 4:18–22). He came to the two on the road to Emmaus (Luke 24:13–27). He came to Saul on the Damascus Road (Acts 9:1–6).

In each intimate relationship revealed by God's Word, our loving Father has been the initiator. Just as He came to sinful people in the person of His Son to redeem us, He now comes to saved people in the person of His Holy Spirit, to indwell us and fill us with intimacy. God is always the initiator of intimacy. We only fail to experience it through disobedience.

As A. W. Tozer said: "We pursue God because, and only because, He has first put an urge within us that spurs us to the pursuit. The impulse to pursue God originates with God, but the outworking of that impulse is our following hard after Him. All the time we are pursuing Him we are already in His hand: 'Thy right hand upholdeth me.'"[7]

It's much easier to find intimacy with God if you do not see yourself as wandering alone along the interstate, deep into the night, without a clue which direction you should go. Instead, see yourself as one loved by God—loved so much He sent His Son to die for you. See yourself as one God continues to love so much that, once you are saved, He pursues you yet to be intimately involved with your life. The heavenly Father didn't pursue you in salvation just to abandon you to a life of cold religion. He comes to you, even now, to stoke the fires of intimacy between you.

God is knowable through the person of Jesus.

Many people struggle with spiritual intimacy because God is a spirit. They ask, "How can I get close to Someone I can't see or talk to face to face?" Getting to know God intimately comes through a relationship with a person, Someone with whom you can become well acquainted. The person of the Godhead you will have the easiest time getting to know is God's Son—Jesus.

While many of your friends may view God as an impersonal distant deity, you know otherwise. God has not stayed away. His desire for intimacy with us prompted Him to assume a body of flesh and dwell among us (John 1:1–3, 14). Jesus was born as a baby in a Bethlehem stable (Luke 2:11). God became a man and lived among other men (Philippians 2:5–8). Jesus experienced every trial and temptation that you and I experience.

Jesus said, "I am the way, the truth, and the life. No one comes to the Father except through Me. If you had known Me, you would have known My Father also; and from now on you know Him and have seen Him" (John 14:6–7). When His disciple Philip questioned how this could be, Jesus simply said, "He who has seen Me has seen the Father" (John 14:9). You can become intimate with the God who is a Spirit by getting to know the God who became flesh.

When a little boy was afraid to go to bed by himself in his dark bedroom, his mother reassured him by saying, "Oh, you're not alone. God is there with you." The frightened boy immediately replied, "That may be true, Mama, but what I need is someone with skin." Well, Jesus Christ is the God with skin. You can enjoy intimacy with the Father by enjoying intimacy with His Son.

How to Develop Intimacy with God

I mentioned above that God initiates a close relationship with us, but this presumes we must also act to foster that intimacy. After all, any vibrant relationship has to have two people intimately relating.

Intimacy requires trust.

We can never be intimate with someone we don't trust. It would be like a spy for one country entering into a meaningful relationship with a spy for another country. So if you want to develop intimacy with God, learn to trust His character. D. L. Moody said, "Character is what you are in the dark." But with God, there is no darkness. "God is light and in Him is no darkness at all" (1 John 1:5). God's character is always the same. He never lies (Titus 1:2); He never goes back on His word (Numbers 23:19); He never changes (James 1:17). His character is absolutely stellar, absolutely perfect, absolutely trustworthy.

You can also learn to trust His faithfulness. A growing concern these days is the failing faithfulness between husbands and wives. Whether it's in the White House or in your house, real intimacy in marriage is only possible with faithfulness in marriage.

When Linda and I said our wedding vows on June 26, 1965, we pledged our love to each other *exclusively*. If I cannot trust my wife's faithfulness to me, I can never allow her out of my sight. And if she cannot trust my faithfulness, she can never permit me to leave her side. What kind of meaningful relationship would that be? The same is true in our relationship with God. He is a faithful lover of His people: "God is love, and he who abides in love abides in God, and God in him" (1 John 4:16). You can develop intimacy with God because He is faithful; His love for you will never be frivolous, it will never fade, it will never fail.

What's more, you can trust that God has your best interests at heart. He wants you to reach your potential in every way. Jeremiah 29:11 records God's promise: "For I know the thoughts that I think toward you, says the LORD, thoughts of peace and not of evil, to give you a future and a hope."

Recently, I preached at a church on the East Coast. After the service a woman came to talk with me about her abusive relationship with her husband, who is now in prison. She showed me horrible scars on her throat and neck, scars left by a pair of scissors and a butcher knife her husband used to try to kill her. What kind of a meaningful relationship could she have with someone who would do that? He certainly didn't have her best interests at heart.

The good news is, our heavenly Father wants nothing but the best for us. He works all things together for our good (Romans 8:28). He will not withhold any good thing from us if we walk blamelessly before Him (Psalm 84:11).

Intimacy requires a right relationship with God.

In space and time, most things are relative. If the center of your city is Fifty-sixth Street and you move from Seventeeth Street to Fortieth Street, obviously you have moved closer to the center of the city. And while that move may have seemed gigantic in relationship to your city, it's nothing in relationship to the world at large. You have not moved materially closer to Paris or Tokyo or Rio de Janeiro.

The same is true with God. Coming closer to God in your relationship may not seem like much when you are contemplating light-years in the galaxies, but it's a huge move when you find your heart drawn closer to His heart. So how do we close the distance? James advises us, "Draw near to God and He will draw near to you" (James 4:8).

That's good advice, but how can we do it? James continues, "Cleanse your hands, you sinners; and purify your hearts, you double-minded.... Humble yourselves in the sight of the Lord, and He will lift you up" (vv. 8, 10).

We can move closer to God by removing any obstacles between us—and sin definitely qualifies as a roadblock. Every time you confess a sin and forsake it, you reduce the distance between God and yourself. Every time you ask God's forgiveness for gossiping about someone at church, you reduce the distance between God and yourself. Every time you humble your pride before God and recognize who He is and who you are, you reduce the distance between your heart and His.

Intimacy requires time.

Building intimacy with God is a lifelong process. It doesn't happen in one church service. You can't read a book on spiritual intimacy and become intimate with God.

I remember well learning this when Linda and I were dating. I wanted to spend as much time with her as I could. Unfortunately, I was attending college three hundred miles from where she was at home. Sometimes months would go by between opportunities to see each other. But when I was home for a weekend or over the Christmas holidays, we were inseparable. Sometimes we would spend sixteen or more hours a day together. To build a meaningful relationship takes time. Anyone who has ever fallen in love knows that.

Yet we often try to build an intimate relationship with God in just an hour on Sunday mornings. We attempt to discover meaning in our life with God by reading a five-minute devotional each day. We want intimacy—we just don't want to pay the price to have it.

But why settle for less than is available to you? What are you willing to do in order to be successful as a Christian? How much time are you willing to spend to become intimate with God? The question is not how much time can you spare. The question is how much intimacy do you want?

Intimacy requires solitude.

When Linda and I were dating, I would come home from college eager to spend time with her. But Linda had four sisters and two brothers, and they would often interrupt our time alone. Her two younger sisters, Kathy and Jodi, loved to climb up on my knee when I came to visit. They could sit and "torture" me for hours. It was difficult to build intimacy in my relationship with Linda while entertaining her younger siblings. What we needed was time alone, and we only got it after my peewee admirers went to bed.

Time alone with God is vital to developing your meaningful relationship with Him. You cannot become intimate with the Father, the Son, or the Holy Spirit while watching television, reading the newspaper, sending e-mails, or engaging in conversation with others. If you really want to develop intimacy with God, you've got to get alone with Him.

That's how the disciples became intimate with Jesus. He told the parable of the sower to the crowds that had gathered along the shores of Galilee, but it was when Jesus was alone with His disciples that they gained insight into the parable. Mark 4:34 says, "But without a parable He did not speak to them. And when they were alone, He explained all things to His disciples." It was when He was alone with His disciples that Jesus asked them, "Who do the crowds say that I am?" (Luke 9:18). That's when Peter developed his intimacy with the Master and it was reflected in his response that Jesus was the Christ of God. You need blocks of time with Jesus Christ to get to know Him.

Intimacy requires stillness.

When I would come home from college to be with Linda, we would often fill our days with activity. We went to a nearby amusement park. We attended church meetings. We spent a Saturday afternoon at the fall Sunday school picnic. Even the times when we were alone, we were busy, always on the go. Eventually we both realized that to get to know each other intimately, we not only needed to be alone, but we also needed to slow down. We couldn't get to know each other while riding the Ferris wheel or driving long distances to events. We needed some quiet nights at home if a meaningful relationship was to develop. We changed our tactics.

If you're having difficulty becoming intimate with God, maybe you need to change your tactics, too. Authors Blackaby and King say, "We are a 'doing' people. We always want to be doing something.... Once in a while someone will say, 'Don't just stand there; do something'.... I think God is crying out and shouting to us, 'Don't just do something. Stand there! Enter into a love relationship with me. Get to know Me. Adjust your life to Me. Let Me love you and reveal Myself to you as I work through you.'"[8]

The next time there is a "must-see" event, stay home. Spend your evening in meaningful *inactivity*. Unplug the television and shut down your computer. If it's even a remote possibility that the phone will ring, turn it off. Find a comfortable chair and simply sit silently before God. I know it's tough, but sit still while you get to know God. It may mean reading your Bible or just meditating on what you've read before. Don't get up and move around. Don't invite others to sit in stillness with you. Make it just God and you.

This is so foreign to us that we may actually fail a few times before we succeed. But shut everything and everybody else out of your world for one night and simply enjoy a meaningful evening with God. Remember what God says: "Be still, and know that I am God" (Psalm 46:10). He didn't write that for Old Testament saints alone. He wrote Psalm 46:10 for you just as much as He wrote John 3:16 for you.

Intimacy requires silence.

It's amazing how couples in love can find such enjoyment just sitting together in silence. They don't need to say anything—just being together is enough. It is as if some deep level of communication takes place that no one else knows or understands. That's certainly the way it was with Linda and me. We would sit in silence, gazing into each other's eyes. Who needed to talk? Our love was growing, and love has a language of its own.

Do you feel that way about your relationship with God? To be successful as a Christian, you need a growing relationship with God, not a static relationship. That kind of relationship requires time to sit alone with Him. You don't have to say a word. In fact, often we express more intimacy without words.

In the preface to his book *The Knowledge of the Holy,* A. W. Tozer laments, "We have lost our spirit of worship and our ability to withdraw inwardly to meet God in adoring silence."[9] The need for solitude and silence has never been greater than it is today. Is it possible that Christians have confused intimacy with praise? Some believers see being intimate with God as closing their eyes, falling into something akin to a spiritual swoon, raising their hands heavenward, and uttering praise phrases. Believe me, I'm all for praising God, but praise alone does not foster intimacy. Much better than just telling God you love Him or singing familiar praises to Him is spending intimate time with Him. Your silent actions speak much louder than your words.

DON'T SETTLE FOR LESS

I feel sorry for Christians who are satisfied to keep their relationship with God on a superficial level. They miss out on so much richness! There is the richness of an ongoing relationship with the God who loves us. There is the richness of knowing Him personally, enjoyably, intimately. That was Paul's desire as a spiritually successful Christian. He pined, "That I may know Him [Christ] and the power of His resurrection, and the fellowship of His sufferings, being conformed to His death" (Philippians 3:10). When we commit to developing an ever-deepening relationship with God, we discover there is so much more than securing our place in heaven when we die. Until you come to the pleasure of intimacy with God, you have only scratched the surface of delight and success.

Make Psalm 16:11 a reality in your life: "You will show me the path of life; in Your presence is fulness of joy; at Your right hand are pleasures forevermore." Between coming to know the path of life in salvation and the eternal pleasures of living with Him forevermore in heaven lies the joy of His continual presence in the Christian life. Get to know that joy. Get to know God intimately. It will make the journey as happy as the destination.

SUCCESS SURVEY #2

1. *Have you felt a need to be closer to God?* Has there been a part of you that still feels distant from Him? Are there little corners of your mind or heart that you have purposefully withheld from Him, claiming them as your private property? Does it bug you that other Christians seem to be more intimate with their Maker? If so, you are in a wonderful position to develop more intimacy with God.

2. *Do you understand and appreciate the biblical metaphors for developing intimacy with God?* Does panting after God or thirsting for Him conjure up the image of what you lack in your relationship with Him? Can you see yourself aching to know God better? Do you feel an urge to become more intimate with Him?

3. *Are you aware that God has a greater desire to be intimate with you than you do with Him?* Have you realized that He even initiates a closer relationship with you? Do you believe that it's possible for finite people like you and me to be deeply in love with a God we can't even see? Do you see Jesus Christ as the tangible God, the God in flesh, the Person of the Godhead who came to earth not only to save you but to make intimacy with God possible? Are you getting to know Him a little better each day?

4. *When things aren't going your way, is your faith strong enough to believe that God has your best interest at heart?* Have you endured a painful event in your life? Did it draw you closer to God or drive you from Him? Did you seek His intimacy during those dark days, or did you try to shut Him out of your life in anger? Do you believe you're ready to develop spiritual intimacy with God? If not, what's holding you back?

5. *Are you willing to make the commitment to do whatever is necessary to become closer to God?* Are you ready to make a time commitment? Are you willing to set some time aside and exclude all others so you can be alone with God? Will you sit still long enough to get to know Him better and to allow Him the opportunity to reveal Himself more intimately to you? Are you ready to take a giant step forward in your relationship with God?

ESTABLISH GOOD GROWTH HABITS

There are some Christians who can't be called pilgrims
because they never make any progress.
ANONYMOUS

But grow in the grace and knowledge of our Lord and Savior Jesus Christ.
2 PETER 3:18

—◦∕◦∕◦—

I t was that day. The day we all dread and put off as long as we can. It was the day of my annual checkup. After hours of poking and prodding, X rays and EKGs, blood pressure and cholesterol checks, it was time for the most embarrassing part of the physical. Well, maybe not *the* most embarrassing part, but certainly the most painful. It was time for my doctor's little heart-to-heart chat. You know the one. Lose weight. Exercise more. Eat better. Try to reduce stress. It was the same speech I had heard dozens of times before, but this time things were going to be different.

I was approaching the years when the AARP and I would become good friends, and now it was time to get serious. I knew I wasn't as young as I used to be, and parts of me where whining every time I summoned their use. I had to establish a healthier lifestyle if I were to accomplish all I felt God had called me to do. But how? What would it take to establish good habits? My doctor claimed he knew.

After some lighthearted banter about my weight, the physician looked me right in the eye and said, "Look, there are only four things that affect your body makeup and weight. The first is heredity, which you can't do anything about. The second is body metabolism, which you can do a little something about. And then there are the big two."

I could see it coming. He was actually going to use the words. I watched his lips and tongue as they formed the syllables.

"Diet and exercise," the doctor blurted out. "The two elements that most contribute to healthy body weight and physical wellness are diet and exercise, and you can control both of them."

There. It was out. The other shoe had dropped. The unwelcome, unsolicited, unpopular duo were thrown right into my face. My physical health, my well-being, and much of my success in the future depended on two things: the disciplines of diet and exercise.

The Importance of Diet and Exercise

As if I had not been convinced by my physician's directions, he sent me to a cardiologist at a local hospital. Nothing serious was wrong; my primary doctor simply wanted a specialist's opinion about my cardiovascular tests. The specialist's name was Dr. Deepak Gangahar, a bright, young Indian heart surgeon with a brilliant future ahead of him.

Dr. Gangahar also gave me a "heart-to-heart" chat about reducing stress and being selective in my diet. He told me to cancel 50 percent of my scheduled speaking engagements and accept 75 percent less in the future. But it was what he said about diet that most caught my attention. The 5-foot, 10-inch, 145-pound physician apparently practiced what he preached—he looked remarkably healthy.

This doctor had been born and raised in India, and his father had died of heart disease. Pursuing a career in medicine, with a specialty in cardiology, seemed to be his way of making sense of his father's death. His mother raised him as an Orthodox Hindu (vegetarian), but when he arrived in the United States in 1971, Dr. Gangahar spent five years indulging in the American way of eating—French fries, hamburgers, milk shakes, and all the other foods that make life worth living. But he knew that had to change as he studied medicine and the effects of diet on the heart.

My talk with Dr. Gangahar convinced me I could eat healthier. I would count calories, watch my fat intake, and consume lots of fruits and vegetables. The exercise part would be a little more difficult because of my travel schedule, but no less important. After all, the Centers for Disease Control estimates that 12 percent of the 250,000 Americans who die every year lack regular exercise, which contributes significantly to their demise.[1] So I determined to watch my diet and make time for exercise, even if it only meant a half-hour walk each day.

On the way home from the hospital, the thought hit me: Diet and exercise not only ensure good physical health, but they ensure good spiritual health as well. To establish good growth habits, we should take in a healthy portion of God's Word and get some spiritual exercise every day. Sounds easy enough, right? Well, just ask anyone who has difficulty maintaining healthy physical habits. It's tough—and good spiritual habits are even tougher to maintain.

So what's the secret to spiritual success? Once you've checked for vital signs and you're certain that you're born again, and once you've begun to develop a thirst for God (even though you haven't completely satisfied it), now it's time to get serious about spiritual growth.

OH, GROW UP

How well I remember those days when Linda and I were raising our children. We welcomed each newborn into our home and treated him or her with kid gloves (no pun intended). There were nighttime feedings (most of which I slept through). There was the white food look-alike called pabulum. And there was baby food—jar after tiny jar of stewed carrots and peas. You haven't lived as a parent until you've worn a layer of green peas splattered all over your face. Now that's an experience!

Linda would put one of our kids in the highchair; I'd pop open a baby food jar; she would get ready; and I'd get the movie camera. There were no video cameras in those days. We had an eight-millimeter camera, the kind that made every home movie look like a Charlie Chaplin film. With a simulated airplane motion, Linda would guide the first bite of green peas into that eager little mouth, and milliseconds later it would be airborne, creating a Picasso-like décor in the kitchen. I would zoom in on Linda's face, splattered with green peas but still smiling good-naturedly.

Babies are cute; they are cuddly; they can do no wrong even when they do wrong. We love them. We overlook their inappropriate bowel behavior. We laugh when they scrunch up their face. We're alarmed at the first sign of a fever. We put up with all the messes they create. Nevertheless, one thing is certain: As much as we love these little ones, we don't want them to stay babies forever.

Newborns may be fun, but they wear on you. There are only so many diapers you can change and still enjoy it. There are only so many times you can strap your baby into a car seat before the novelty wears off. And there are only so many times you can wipe up a mess from the kitchen floor and maintain patience. After a while, we want our babies to grow up and care for themselves.

It's the same way with spiritual newborns. We all rejoice when someone is born into the kingdom of God. We rush to their side. We overlook their faults and answer their questions. We want to help them drink in the milk of the Word so they may grow (1 Peter 2:2). But how long should the spiritually newborn drink milk without taking in solid food? How long should the born again person remain a spiritual babe?

Too many Christians today are stuck in spiritual infancy. They are alive in Christ, but they have never grown. When offered the meat of the Word, they are more than content with pabulum. As someone once said, "You are young only once, but you can stay immature indefinitely." If you want to be a spiritual success, one of the secrets is to establish good growth habits so you can grow out of spiritual infancy as soon as possible. It all comes back to diet and exercise.

EAT A BALANCED SPIRITUAL DIET

The hungriest prophet I know was Jeremiah. He said, "Your words were found, and I ate them, and Your word was to me the joy and rejoicing of my heart" (Jeremiah 15:16). That's a strange concept—eating the Word of God. Or is it? Why should we not crave the best food possible for our spiritual growth? Why should the person who needs to grow strong spiritual muscles and bones not devour the nutrients of the Word?

If a balanced diet is one of the keys to being physically fit, it's also one of the keys to being spiritually fit. Eating a balanced diet means getting proper amounts of the five basic Bible food groups:

History—books like Genesis, Joshua, 1 Samuel, and Acts
Prophecy—books like Daniel, Revelation, Ezekiel, and Jeremiah
Poetry—books like Psalms, Proverbs, Ecclesiastes, and Song of Solomon
Gospel—books like Matthew, Mark, Luke, and John
Epistles—books like Romans, Ephesians, 1 Peter, and Jude

You may not need to eat from these five groups every day, but you do need to eat regularly from all five if you want a healthy spiritual diet. Eating a balanced diet means ingesting what you need, not just what you want.

Green beans or Gummi Bears?

A growing number of Christians today have developed a taste for spiritual junk food. I suppose spiritual junk food is better than no food at all, but it's not a balanced, vitamin-enriched diet. If you munch only tasty, sweet candy to the exclusion of vitamin-packed lean meat and vegetables, you will find yourself stuck in spiritual infancy. What the Christian needs are green beans, but what a lot of Christians want are Gummi Bears.

Let's face it, Gummi Bears are tasty, cute, squishy, brightly colored, and convenient. They've got everything going for them—except food value. On the other hand, green beans are less tasty; they're not so cute; nobody likes them squishy; and they are not brightly colored. The main thing green beans have going for them is their nutritional value. They will help make you strong and healthy. Eating Gummi Bears is a nice treat, but eating green beans is what establishing good growth habits is all about.

When you study God's Word, don't settle for Gummi Bears. When you buy study books on the Word, don't settle for Gummi Bears. When you listen to Christian radio or watch Christian television, check out how much of the content is based on the Bible. When buying Christian books, look for references to the Word. If they are scarce, the fare may be tasty, but is it what you need to grow?

Man does not live by principles alone.

A friend of mine told me about his brother-in-law, a highly skilled physician named Fred. He is respected in his field and board certified in his area of specialty—neurology. Fred reads all the latest medical summaries, but he maintains such a busy schedule that he never has time to "wade into the details." Fred frequently secures a synopsis of the latest medical research because there just isn't time to do all that intense reading. My friend told me that Fred's patients think he's on top of the latest medical developments, and to some extent he is. Yet sometimes he finds himself in trouble in a case because, while he is familiar with the general overview of a specific medical problem, he had failed to dig in to all the details.

Sometimes that happens to us. Often we skim the Bible and try to live by broad, general principles. In fact, sometimes we read God's Word only to discover little nuggets of truth. When we read books or listen to sermons, we filter out the specifics and take away only the outline of the message. But when we seek only the big-picture, sweeping principles, we risk missing the substance of Scripture.

When Jesus was tempted by Satan in the wilderness and elsewhere, He responded to each temptation by quoting Scripture. Once He said, "Man shall not live by bread alone, but by every word that proceeds from the mouth of God" (Matthew 4:4). When God inspired the writers of Scripture with the thoughts and words of His mind, He said exactly what He wanted to say. The specific words of Scripture are important—not just the concepts of Scripture.

In 1996, Tyndale House Publishers commissioned a national survey, "Bible Reading in America," which was conducted by the respected Barna Research Group. The survey discovered that 86 percent of American adults claimed to know the basic principles of the Bible "somewhat" or "very well," but a large percentage performed poorly on a basic quiz of Bible knowledge.[2]

When you study God's Word, don't just skim the highlights to gain some principles. Look closely at the words. Dissect the language to understand the specifics. Get down to the nitty-gritty of the biblical ideas. Henry Ford said, "Cut your own wood and you warm yourself twice." Don't rely on second-hand principles taught to you by someone else. Simple biblical principles are fine, but they often enslave Christians to spiritual immaturity.

Howard Hendricks tells of visiting Yellowstone National Park and being handed a sheet of paper by a ranger at the park entrance. The paper warned, "Do

Not Feed the Bears." But as soon as Hendricks drove into the park, he saw people feeding the bears everywhere. When he asked a ranger about it, the ranger said, "You have only a small part of the picture." Then the ranger described how the park service personnel in the fall and winter have to carry away the carcasses of dead bears...bears that have lost their ability to find food for themselves because they've become dependent on people's handouts.

When Christians rely solely on others for their spiritual sustenance, they risk becoming unfit and anemic. There is an easy solution to this problem. Open your Bible and go exploring for yourself. Seek out the substance beyond the basic principles. God has things to say to you, but you'll miss them if you search only for the tasty dessert portions of Scripture while skipping the meat and potatoes.

Substance, not just application

When I teach God's Word on radio or television, I always endeavor to establish three things—what the Word says, what the Word means by what it says, and how the Word applies to the lives of my listeners. These three things are the basics of Bible study.

The third millennium after Christ will be characterized by a "cut-to-the-chase" mentality. This escalated in the eighties and nineties of the second millennium, when computers and the media increased the amount of information available to us and the speed to which we could access it. Now we want to get to the bottom line as fast as we can. Often that happens in Bible study. We want to get to application without a foundation in substance and interpretation. Said another way, we see Bible study as answering the question, "How does it apply to me?" But that question cannot be answered in a lasting and meaningful way without first addressing what the Word says and means.

Before you can move on from spiritual infancy, you must get a grip on what's in the Bible. I call this the "stuff" of the Bible (pardon the use of such a technical term). What is the stuff of God's Word? All the foundational material. All the background that helps add precision to our reading of the Bible. All the names, places, and events that inform our understanding of biblical guidelines. Who is Abraham, and did he live before or after Moses? How does Psalms differ from the historical books? What does Romans have to say about how salvation works? Who are David, Lot, Timothy, Aaron, Ruth, and James? What are the important truths of Scripture that, if applied appropriately, will impact my life? This is all the head information we need before it can be transformed into heart inspiration.

Is "stuff" enough?

As important as knowing the stuff of Scripture is, it's not enough to change your life. Nikita Krushchev, the shoe-pounding former premier of the USSR, reportedly could quote large portions of Scripture from memory. Apparently when he was a child, his grandmother would give him a piece of candy for each verse he could recite. As a result, Krushchev knew a lot of stuff from the New Testament. But it seems as if no lasting benefit was gained by just knowing the stuff.

Discovering facts, identifying people and places, or grappling with doctrinal truths isn't enough. Until we interpret the things we read in Scripture and apply what the Bible says to our lives, we have just been on a fact-finding mission. It's a bit like Lucy saying to Charlie Brown: "I just completed a course in speed reading and last night I read *War and Peace* in one hour!… It was about Russia." No, you need more than stuff. If all you have are facts, then, like Lucy, you might simplistically conclude that the Bible is about Israel. You and I need more than knowledge about the stuff of Scripture.

In his book *No Place for Truth,* David Wells addresses the issue of people having all the biblical facts down pat, but failing to do anything with them. He asks, "What does it mean, for example, when 91 percent of evangelicals say that their beliefs are 'very important' to them, when 93 percent say that they believe in divine judgment, when 96 percent say that they believe in miracles? It does not necessarily mean all that much. Even in churches that are active and among believers who are religiously observant, it is possible that theology…has become peripheral and remote."[3]

The catchy phrase "Life, not doctrine" that has been the slogan of American liberal churches betrays a ruinous sacrifice of what the Bible says and what it means on the altar of application. We need to absorb the doctrines of the Word, not just the principles of the Word. Understanding theology requires interpretation of what the Bible says. We cannot apply what we do not understand. That's why the middle interpretation step is so important, and sometimes we may need a pastor or mentor to help us interpret what we read.

Growing strong spiritually doesn't happen any more rapidly than growing strong physically does. It is a lifetime project. We'll never mature in the faith if we skip important growth habits such as studying the Word daily to find out what's in there and then seeking to understand what we read before we try to apply it.

Taking responsibility

J. I. Packer was right when he wrote in the foreword to R. C. Sproul's *Knowing Scripture:* "If I were the devil, one of my first aims would be to stop folk from digging into the Bible…. I should do all I could to surround it with the spiritual equivalent of pits, throne hedges, and man traps, to frighten people off."[4] What Packer believes he would do if he were the devil is precisely what Satan has already done. If you want to be spiritually successful, it's time for you to take personal responsibility for digging into the Bible.

There are lots of books available to teach you how to study your Bible, but none of them will make you do it. If you want to work out a good, nutritious diet for your own spiritual growth, it's not your pastor's responsibility to do it for you. It's not your spouse's responsibility or your small group leader's responsibility. Your spiritual growth is *your* responsibility. You can get lots of help, but making the decision to move on from spiritual infancy to spiritual maturity is a personal decision.

When my doctor had his little heart-to-heart chat with me about good growth habits, he laid the burden squarely on me to help myself. He could give me advice, but I had to act on it. My wife could prepare low-fat meals, but I had to shun junk food. I am the one who had to practice healthy living. Spiritually, you are the one who decides if you drink milk the rest of your life or move on to more substantial food.

Pastor and Bible teacher John MacArthur knows the value of personally digging into the Word for meat and not just for milk. He says, "The greatest thing that ever happened in my life, next to my salvation, occurred when I learned to study the Word of God night and day. While I haven't arrived, by any stretch of the imagination, I have learned this—that the longer and more intensely and more devotedly I look into the face of God, the more God changes my life into the image of His Son."[5]

Develop an insatiable appetite. Don't settle for Gummi Bears. Go for the green beans. Read until you look into the face of God. Take responsibility for your own spiritual health.

THE IMPORTANCE OF SPIRITUAL EXERCISE

Maintaining a good spiritual diet, one that will ensure spiritual growth, is much easier than maintaining a good exercise program. But as I learned—and as doctors, nutritionists, and personal trainers have been saying for years—diet alone is not enough. You need both diet and exercise if you are to be healthy.

Output is equally important as intake. If you want to lose weight, you have to reduce your fat and calorie intake while you increase burning those calories. And you know what that means—exercise, exertion, activity.

I'll admit that I don't enjoy exercise. I do it—I just don't like it. I've heard people talk about "runner's high" and the euphoria that comes with prolonged physical activity, but I've never experienced it. What's more, I'd be more convinced that runner's high exists if I saw smiles on the faces of those sweaty joggers rather than strained grimaces.

It's difficult to maintain an exercise regimen when you do it only because you know you should. And often we neglect spiritual exercise for the same reason. We feel we ought to do it, but it's not something we look forward to. We have a sense of obligation, but not a sense of anticipation.

Spiritual exercise means we put feet to our Bible study. We should never study the Bible for the sake of becoming a Bible student. We do it to grow so that we may be more fit as servants of the One who loved us and gave Himself for us (Ephesians 5:2). Spiritual exercise is the secret to strong spiritual muscles and bones. What follows are just a few of the ways we exercise our faith and in the process become stronger and more successful.

The exercise of prayer

It seems as if there are as many books about prayer available today as people to read them. The church talks a lot about prayer, but I'm not convinced church members do a lot of praying.

When researchers with the Gallup organization surveyed Americans regarding the role of prayer in their lives, they discovered that 82 percent of the female respondents said prayer was important, and 69 percent of the men said it was important.[6] But while a pretty high percentage of people say prayer is important to them, there isn't much evidence that they believe what they say. Dallas Willard must have observed the same thing. He said, "The 'open secret' of many 'Bible-believing' churches is that a vanishing small percentage of those talking about prayer...are actually doing what they are talking about."[7]

There has been a great prayer movement during the last decade, and we hope it has reversed this "open secret." But the jury is still out. Why do people who say prayer is important do so little praying? Maybe it's because prayer is much harder work than most of us would like to admit.

How hard is prayer?

If you've never wrestled with God in prayer, you don't know just how hard this work is. Luke 22:44 tells us that Jesus "prayed more earnestly. Then His sweat became like great drops of blood falling down to the ground." I'm sure there have been many times when you've worked so hard that you sweat profusely. But have you ever broken into a sweat while praying? If you think prayer isn't hard work, when you get to heaven, ask Jesus about it.

Do you think prayer was easy for Jonah in the belly of that great fish (Jonah 2:1–10)? Was it easy for Elijah, who faced death and defeat at the hands of the wicked Queen Jezebel and her prophets of Baal (1 Kings 18:36–37)? Was prayer easy for King Hezekiah when Jerusalem was surrounded by Assyrian King Sennacherib's mighty army (2 Kings 19:15–19)?

Sometimes prayer is an act of the will. That is, we know it's the right thing to do, but it's not easy or pleasant. Just ask Lisa. She never dreamed she would become a battered wife when she first married. After all, her husband, Tom, was a highly respected Christian, a successful businessman, and an active member of their church. During their courtship, Lisa and Tom often prayed and read God's Word together. At times she saw him lose his temper, but she assumed that was just one of those areas Tom was struggling with. She spent many an hour praying for him—until the day when, in a fit of rage, Tom knocked out two of her teeth and blackened her eye. After that, the incidents came with increasing frequency, and Lisa found it more and more difficult to pray for Tom. "I really tried," she finally confided to her pastor when she called him from a shelter for battered women. "I think Tom's sincere, but I'm just agonized about how to pray for him. After all, I've prayed about this for the entire two years we've been married—and things have only gotten worse. But even though it's tough to keep praying, I know I should continue...and I will."

For those like Lisa who take prayer seriously, the exercise is made even more difficult when people talk as if prayer were unimportant. I have heard well-meaning preachers say things that must have made prayer warriors feel like third-class citizens. They've said things like, "Well, if you can't support our missionaries financially, you can at least pray for them." Or, "If you can't go on this outreach, you can always pray." What kind of foolishness is that? Anybody can give, and almost anybody can go, but I don't know many people who can pray well. The exercise of prayer is one of the major disciplines that helps us be successful in our Christian lives.

Roadblocks to success

Is your prayer life a bit anemic? Does it sometimes seem like God isn't listening when you pray? The problem is not with God. Prayer is successful when our attitudes are right. Often the attitudes we adopt when we pray become roadblocks to our success. We must come to God with the attitude of privilege. After all, look who it is that invites us to pray (Jeremiah 33:3). Look in whose authority we come to the Father in prayer (John 14:13–14). Look in whose help we engage in prayer (Romans 8:26). What a privilege! But the attitude of privilege must be tempered with the attitude of humility. If we come to God the same way the proud Pharisee did in Jesus' story of the tax collector, we'll go away from God empty-handed the way the Pharisee did (Luke 18:10–14). Attitude is everything.

Once you've checked your attitude, see if you've set up any other roadblocks to your success. For example, Psalm 66:18 warns, "If I regard iniquity in my heart, the Lord will not hear." If there is a little corner of your mind that you refuse to submit to the Lord, a little sin you know is wrong, that will be a deterrent to your success in prayer. Other deterrents are asking for the wrong things or asking with the wrong motives (Matthew 20:20–23; James 4:3). Roadblocks also can be erected when we have a faulty relationship with God or with others (Jeremiah 7:16; Matthew 5:23–24).

The sky is not the limit.

Nothing is beyond the bounds of prayer. If you want to be successful in spiritual living, pray about everything. Don't categorize your prayers into "big" requests and "trivial" requests. Anything big enough to take to God is a big request.

Just as you did in finding a time and a place to read God's Word, do the same with prayer. Pray with others, but find some time to get alone and pray, perhaps as part of your Bible study time. I find it meaningful to spend time talking with God after He has spent time talking with me through His Word. My time with God each day, my spiritual strength regimen, consists of a third of the time reading God's Word, a third of the time talking with Him in prayer, and a third of the time in quiet contemplation and listening to God. It's during this "third third" that I have found myself drawn in intimacy to God.

Prayer is a discipline. It's not just sending a shopping list up to God and saying, "Gimme, gimme." It's a time of communion with God. It's a time of intimacy with God. It's a time of worship to God. And, yes, it's a time of request to God, but prayer does take time and anything that takes time takes discipline. Develop a prayer rapport with God that brings you into His intimate presence both on spontaneous occasions and on regularly scheduled occasions.

THE EXERCISE OF CHURCH ATTENDENCE

Many of us remember when attending church was not an event but an exercise of spiritual discipline. Let's face it, over the last quarter of the twentieth century, the local church has changed dramatically.

Many people today belong to a "megachurch," which is a church so large that traditional methods of fellowship have had to be altered to make way for new methods of fellowship. The pastor doesn't greet us at the door anymore. (Parishioners scurry out a dozen doors, and the pastor has not mastered the art of omnipresence.) We don't call out our favorite hymns by number in the hymnal so we can sing what we choose. Audiences aren't solicited for requests anymore because the power-point program is preset long before the service, and we don't have hymnals anyway. Church has changed.

For those of my generation, for all who don't necessarily like these changes, for those who long for the "good old days," there's bad news: We aren't going back. We can't go back. Music and worship styles continue to evolve and usually drive change in the church rather than respond to it.

So, okay, church is different. It's still church. The local church is one of three entities established by God (government and the family being the other two), and it will always be His church. Jesus solemnly promised, "On this rock I will build My church, and the gates of Hades shall not prevail against it" (Matthew 16:18). The church of which Jesus spoke is not the building you meet in on Sunday but the body of believers to which you belong. That body is made up of all races, all nationalities, all sexes, all political persuasions, all peoples washed clean by the blood of the Lamb.

That church is universal, made up of all those "called out" of the world. (That's the meaning of the word *church—ekklesia* or called out from others.) But the only way this universal church can function is to meet together in local assemblies. We should always see ourselves as belonging to a group larger than our local congregation, but we should never see ourselves as belonging to that larger group if we are not disciplined enough to be a part of a local congregation.

What difference does it make if you identify with a particular local body of believers or just live your Christian life as a lone ranger? The difference is discipline. President Theodore Roosevelt reminded us, "You may worship God anywhere, at any time, but the chances are that you will not do so unless you have first learned to worship Him in some particular place, and at some particular time."[8] We go to church as a discipline of spiritual growth.

What is church for?

Don't think of church as the place you go to get a blessing, but as the place you go to *be* a blessing. Don't think of church just as the place you learn God's Word, but as the place you get your spiritual batteries recharged. Don't think of church so much as the place you learn to be a soldier, but as the place you go to get your marching orders.

You can study God's Word at home, and you should. You can pray in your car, and you should. You can learn how to be a soldier from a Bible conference, and you should. But you cannot identify with the people of God and live in obedience to the commands of Christ without being a part of a local church.

Christ gave to His church various gifted people to assist the body in our search for spiritual success. These people were given "for the equipping of the saints for the work of the ministry" and "for the edifying of the body of Christ" (Ephesians 4:12). It couldn't be plainer: The twofold ministry of the church in your life is equipping and edifying.

When the writer of Hebrews said, "Let us hold fast the confession of our hope without wavering" (10:23), he wasn't asking us to be a lone sentinel at our post. When he said, "Let us consider one another in order to stir up love and good works" (10:24), he wasn't suggesting we do this on our own. And when he said, "Not forsaking the assembling of ourselves together" (10:25), he wasn't encouraging regular attendance at a ball game. Willful neglect of church attendance brings a "certain fearful expectation of judgment" (10:27). That's how important church attendance is.

Why go to church?

With a light spiritual diet and diminishing personal discipline, many Christians have decided that attending church is not important. *U.S. News and World Report* says that eight of every ten Americans today believe that it's possible to be a good Christian or Jew even without attending a church or synagogue.[9] Increasing numbers of people are either staying away from church or simply identifying with church at arm's length. With larger congregations today, it's easy to say you attend such-and-such church while remaining anonymous. No one there has ever heard of you.

Robert W. Patterson, with the National Association of Evangelicals, expressed his concern about the failure of Christians to identify with a local church. He said:

> When President Dwight Eisenhower became a Christian, he made a public profession of faith in Christ, was baptized, and was extended the right hand of fellowship at the national Presbyterian Church in Washington, D.C., the second Sunday after his inauguration in 1953. Had the former President expressed interest in becoming a Christian a generation later under more consciously evangelical auspices, he might never have been challenged to identify with the body of Christ through baptism and church membership. A personal relationship with Jesus, he would have been told, is all that really matters.[10]

So why go to church? People go for different reasons. Some parents go to be an example to their children. That's good and important. *Leadership* magazine reported a study that in homes where both Mom and Dad attend church regularly, 72 percent of their children remain faithful in attendance. If only Dad attends regularly, 55 percent remain faithful. If only Mom attends regularly, 15 percent remain faithful. If neither attend regularly, only 6 percent remain faithful.[11]

Others go to church because it's a great place to network. They meet business associates there. It's part of the social scene in their community. Still others go for purely personal reasons. They simply feel better when they attend church. *Time* magazine reported a study by the National Institute on Aging showing that of four thousand elderly people living at home in North Carolina, the vast majority who attended church experienced much greater physical and mental well-being than those who didn't attend church.[12]

But there are much better reasons than these to attend church. We go to worship God. We go to praise the name of Jesus. We go to fellowship with others and to exhort one another. If we simply go to church to "get a blessing," we'll likely not go long. Church attendance is one of those disciplines of the Christian life that proves we are moving toward spiritual maturity. What God uses to develop our maturity is also one of the evidences that we have gained maturity.

Sometimes we go to church simply because it's a way to say to the world that we belong to the Savior. We go because we know it's the right thing to do. I heard about a little old man who could be seen every Sunday morning walking to church. But he was deaf, so he could not hear a word of the sermon or the music. Someone asked him, "Why do you spend your Sundays in that church when you can't hear a word?" He replied, "I want my neighbors to know which side I'm on!" Go to church as a testimony to a watching world and out of genuine love for the Savior.

THE EXERCISE OF WITNESSING

Do you know what the first recorded words of Jesus were? They are found in the second chapter of Luke. Joseph and Mary, who had left their son in the Temple and discovered Him missing, returned to Jerusalem to find Him. When they located Him, Mary said, "Son, why have You done this to us? Look, Your father and I have sought you anxiously" (2:48). Then Jesus, just twelve years old at the time, replied: "Why did you seek Me? Did you not know that I must be about My Father's business?" Before any teaching about the kingdom, before any advice on prayer, before calling His twelve disciples or predicting His death, Jesus said, "I must be about My Father's business."

Do you remember what the last words of Jesus were? The last recorded words of our Lord are found in Acts 1:8. After he had been crucified and raised from the dead, and just before He ascended to heaven, Jesus said to His disciples, "But you shall receive power when the Holy Spirit has come upon you; and you shall be witnesses to Me in Jerusalem, and in all Judea and Samaria, and to the end of the earth."

How interesting that Jesus' first words were a declaration that *He* should be about His Father's business and His last words were a declaration that *we* should be about His Father's business. Aren't you challenged by that notion? This helps us identify one of the most significant areas in which a spiritual exercise program is needed to help us to spiritual maturity.

Witnessing and evangelism

But you may say, "Wait a minute. Isn't winning the lost the business of the church? Don't we have crusades and revivals to do that? Isn't that what men like Billy Graham and Luis Palau do?" The answer is yes to all of the above. But witnessing is a personal matter, too.

There is a difference between witnessing and evangelism. Paul challenged Timothy to "do the work of an evangelist" in order to "fulfill your ministry" (2 Timothy 4:5). Some people, like Timothy, are specifically called by God to be evangelists, and when God calls He also gifts and equips. There is a need today for individuals to answer the call of God to be evangelists just as there is the need for individuals to answer God's call to be pastors (Ephesians 4:11).

But beyond that specific call, God has designed each of us to be witnesses. Jesus said to the crowd of disciples who had gathered at His ascension, "You shall be witnesses to Me" (Acts 1:8). That wasn't a specific call to evangelism, but it was a specific statement of fact. Saved people are to be witnesses of their salvation. Witnessing is not for the specifically gifted; witnessing is for those who have something to witness about.

Recently the American Institute of Church Growth surveyed some eight thousand people to learn why they came to church. Here's what they learned: One to 2 percent came because they responded to a church visitation program; 2 to 3 percent were walk-ins; 5 to 6 percent were influenced by the preacher; and there were some other small percentage reasons. Do you want to guess what percentage of people came to church because they were influenced by friends or relatives? A whopping 75 to 90 percent.[13] Is it any wonder that God calls each of us to be a witness to His grace?

When I witness about my faith in Jesus Christ, I always have the intention of doing the work of an evangelist. I give the facts and call for a conclusion. What Jesus did for me in saving me, He can do for the one I'm witnessing to. But I can't draw that person to the Lord; that's the work of the Father through the Holy Spirit (John 6:44). And I can't make that person believe; that's his or her responsibility (John 3:14–17). My responsibility? Be a witness. And that's your responsibility, too.

Gotta tell somebody

I've seen what Jesus can do in changing a life forever, and I'm just like those shepherds who went to see the baby Jesus lying in the manger: "Now when they had seen Him, they made widely known the saying which was told them concerning this Child" (Luke 2:17).

I'm like Andrew after he was introduced to the Lamb of God who takes away the sin of the world (John 1:29). I'm tracking down my brother to tell him, "We have found the Messiah" (John 1:41).

I'm just like Philip when he encountered Jesus for the first time, and Jesus said to him, "Follow Me." I'm out looking for my buddy to say to him, "We have found Him of whom Moses in the law, and also the prophets, wrote—Jesus of Nazareth, the son of Joseph" (John 1:45).

I'm like the woman at the well who, having encountered Jesus Christ in a meaningful way, announced to her city, "Come, see a Man who told me all things that I ever did. Could this be the Christ?" (John 4:29).

I'm like the women at the empty tomb who saw the risen Christ and then "returned from the tomb and told all these things to the eleven and to all the rest" (Luke 24:9).

I'm like the two on the road to Emmaus who were joined by the resurrected Jesus and had the Scriptures opened to them. Once He vanished from their sight, "they rose up that very hour and returned to Jerusalem...and they told about the things that had happened on the road" (Luke 24:33–35).

I'm a witness because I've witnessed a change in my own life. I'm not a witness because I have received the call of an evangelist. I'm not a witness because I'm exercising the gift of evangelism. I'm a witness because things have happened in my life that only God could do. Now I'm in the company of the shepherds, Andrew, Philip, the woman at the well, the women at the tomb, and Cleopas and his friend on the Emmaus Road. I'm in pretty good company as a witness.

Witnessing isn't difficult. It's just telling the truth about what happened to us. I tell the truth to lead people to the One who is the Truth. That's a spiritual discipline that every Christian can exercise.

THE BOTTOM LINE

There's so much more that could be said about establishing good spiritual growth habits. But the bottom line is this: Babies are born not to stay helpless and dependent, but to grow and mature. Growth takes the right combination of diet and exercise. Spiritual growth also takes the right combination of diet and exercise.

For you and me to move beyond spiritual infancy and grow toward spiritual maturity, we need much more than milk and baby food. We need the deep things of God's Word, the meat. To be spiritually healthy we have to avoid a steady diet of Gummi Bears and exchange them for a steady diet of green beans. You won't find green beans in the candy section of your grocery store, and you won't find solid spiritual food in all that sugary sweet stuff that is packaged for spiritual lightweights.

To be spiritually successful, exercise daily. Exercise your right to pray directly to God through the name of Jesus and in the power of the Holy Spirit. Exercise your gifts at church and contribute to the lives of others. Exercise your freedom of speech by telling others of the wonderful Person who has changed your life. Establish a spiritual regimen and stick with it to stay spiritually fit.

The alternative? You could be a spiritual weakling all your life, whining every time Satan kicks sand in your face. But that's no way to live, not when Jesus promised you abundant life (John 10:10). Tap into the good growth habits of that abundant life and see what a difference it makes for you.

Dr. Deepak Gangahar gave me good advice when he said I needed to change my diet and exercise regularly. I have followed his advice for the past several years, and there's no doubt that I am healthier. I have more energy, stamina, and endurance than I did before. What's more, I have applied the same principles to my spiritual life and found that there, too, I am healthier. I now have more vitality in my walk with the Lord. I am enjoying better spiritual health because I have learned to establish good growth habits. You can do the same thing.

SUCCESS SURVEY #3

1. *Has your spiritual growth been all you want it to be?* Or are you stuck in spiritual infancy? Do you desire to grow and mature but feel stalled in your current level of development? It doesn't have to be that way. Does it seem like you are no closer to being like Jesus now than the day you trusted Him as Savior? Does that trouble you? Be honest.

2. *What does your spiritual diet look like?* Are you consuming only spiritual junk food? Have you moved beyond the stories like David and Goliath and sunk your teeth into some of the great doctrines of the Scripture? The old Bible stories are wonderful, but if that's all you gain from God's Word, you are just settling and surviving. God has so much more for you. Are you still sipping the milk of the Word? What will it be—Gummi Bears or green beans? Only you can decide.

3. *Do you feed yourself—or do you rely on others for sustenance?* Do you discipline yourself to spend time in God's Word each day? Are you still getting all your spiritual growth from what others are teaching you, or have you rolled up your sleeves and begun to dig into God's Word yourself? Are you trying to grow strong in the Lord on simple principles you find in the Bible, or are you eating up big chunks of the Word itself? Each of us must feed ourselves and be responsible for our spiritual growth.

4. *What spiritual exercises are you best at?* Has a vital prayer life always been a dream, something others are good at but not you? Do you feel God isn't paying attention when you pray? What are the roadblocks that stand in the way of your success in prayer? How will you get rid of those roadblocks? God's Word provides a road map for blasting away roadblocks.[14]

5. *If you were filling out a questionnaire that asked what church you belonged to, would you have an answer?* If those sponsoring the questionnaire checked with others in that church, would they know who you are? When was the last time you gave of your talents to serve that church? Are you an impact player or a bench warmer? And what about telling others about Jesus? Could you guide someone into an eternal relationship with God? Spiritual growth is all about growing, and that means diet and exercise. Are you getting enough?

SPIRITUAL SECRET #4

ENLIST SUPERIOR HELP

He who sees a need and waits to be asked for help
is as unkind as if he had refused it.
DANTE

Our help is in the name of the LORD, who made heaven and earth.
PSALM 124:8

—◦◦◦—

His name was Dr. Paul Griffis, but many people knew him simply as "Uncle Paul." He was one of the most meaningful mentors in my life. I loved that man.

I first met Dr. Griffis when I was a teenager. He was the academic dean at Practical Bible Training School (now Practical Bible College) in Binghamton, New York. Dr. Griffis was a frequent speaker at Bible conferences in the East, and my father invited him to our little church for a conference. Dr. Griffis was tall, thin, and had a beautiful head of white hair. He was a stately man, but much more importantly, he was a godly man.

Over the years, I observed him preach many times, and I never saw him open his Bible. Don't misunderstand—it's not that he didn't preach the Word. In fact, he knew the Bible so well that he could speak on a passage from memory. He would hold his Bible in his hand and say something like, "Today I want you to think with me about Paul's instructions to the Colossians in chapter 3." He would then quote the entire passage from memory. He was amazing! I used to follow along in my Bible just to see if he ever missed a word. He didn't.

He was partly the reason I decided as a young teenager to attend the institution where he taught. I wanted to be like him.

Dr. Griffis wasn't just a teacher—he was an *excellent* teacher. He taught me the Greek language and much more. He was also a Christian innovator. For many years, he had pastored the Little White Church near Binghamton. This church's modest name belied its vast influence. It was a major work for God. Dr. Griffis also founded the Arrowhead Bible Camp in Brackney, Pennsylvania. There, thousands of boys and girls came for summer camp, and hundreds of them trusted Jesus Christ as their Savior.

But Paul Griffis wasn't finished. He knew the area needed a Christian bookstore, so he started the Arrowhead Christian Center to provided literature and educational materials for churches and individuals. Dr. Griffis invented a looseleaf Bible, which later was purchased by Fleming H. Revell Publishing Company. It enabled a pastor or teacher to place a page of notes in his Bible and remove them after his message. It was a brilliant concept.

Paul Griffis was the entire Christian package—husband, father, scholar, leader, Christian gentleman. But more than this, he was my friend and mentor. While in school, my first class of the day was his Greek course. Dr. Griffis was blue-green color blind and would often show up for that class wearing odd color combinations. Almost daily he would come over to where I sat and ask in a soft voice, "Does this tie match this suit?"

As a student, I would sometimes travel with him to lead singing before he taught the Word. I suppose I learned more from observing his life off campus than I did from attending his classes. From him I learned that being a scholar, a godly gentleman, a family man, and a friend was not too much to ask of any one person. He always had time for everyone. He was always there for me when I needed advice, encouragement, correction, or direction.

Of all the things that Dr. Griffis taught me, one thing stands out among the rest: Christians who want to achieve spiritual success need other believers to guide, support, and encourage them. The Christian life was never meant to be lived in isolation. I need others to be successful, just as they need me. Success depends on our being there for one another when we are most likely to fail.

This concept is woven throughout the New Testament. The apostle Paul used the analogy of a body to demonstrate how interdependent we are with our Christian brothers and sisters. You can read all about it in 1 Corinthians 12:12–19. God never intended for you to face the trials of life alone. He has placed others in a position to assist you. So enlist help as often as you need it. But make sure you enlist superior help, because not everyone is equally qualified or gifted to make you be successful. What kind of superior help has God given you? Here are some of the categories of helpers who can enable you to be successful in your Christian life.

ENLIST THE HELP OF FRIENDS

When an English publication offered a prize for the best definition of a friend, thousands of people entered. One prize winner was this: "A friend is someone who multiplies joys and divides grief." Another top entry said, "A friend is some-one who understands our silence." But the first-place definition was, "A friend is someone who comes in when the whole world has gone out."

Friends have been the stuff of which many a standup comic has made his living: If you really want your friends to remember you, give them something cheap. But friends are no laughing matter. Friends can make us or break us. They can be the joy of our life. C. S. Lewis once mused, "Is any pleasure on earth as great as a circle of Christian friends by a fire?"

Not long ago my local newspaper ran a feature story entitled, "Friends for Life." It described the lifelong friendship of three Camp Fire Girls who met during the Great Depression. Fern was an athlete. Virginia was the shortest girl in class. Dorothy had a sharp memory. They giggled their way through their teen years. They helped each other through school. They sealed their friendship with chocolate caramel sundaes. And now, more than fifty years later, Fern Heim, Dorothy Blackburn, and Virginia Manke remain lifelong friends. Every couple of years they meet to sing old Camp Fire Girls songs and catch up on their grand-children.

As Dorothy explains, "Old friends see each other as they really are—see things as they really were. You have that special feeling, you understand each other so much better because you've had the same experiences, teachers, goals."

Eventually the three girls grew up, and their lives moved in different directions.

"Even though you have a close friendship, you begin to go your separate ways," Fern said. But when they get together, reminiscences run high.

"There was a lot of 'Whatever happened to…?'" Virginia said. "We shared snapshots and pictures of families, talked about old students and friends."

Getting together isn't as easy as it used to be. While Fern continues to live in Lincoln, Nebraska; Dorothy now lives in San Antonio, Texas; and Virginia resides in Fort Collins, Colorado. But for these "friends for life," time and distance are not insurmountable obstacles.[1]

Friendship is not a gift; it's earned every day. We invest a great deal of our life in our friends. Here are some reasons why they are so important as helpers.

Friends are available when we need them.

One reason friends have such influence on our success is that we have a unique relationship with them—a different kind of relationship than we have with relatives. Someone has said, "God gives us our relatives; thank heaven we can choose our friends."

While blood is thicker than water, it often has less impact. Frequently relatives are far away, living in distant towns or countries. We can always call or e-mail them, but friends are often close at hand. As Proverbs 27:10 says, "Better is a neighbor nearby than a brother far away." Friends are right there when we need advice. They are there for us when we need help. Friends can be more immediate than families, and therefore they are often more helpful in our spiritual success.

In his book *Kingdoms in Conflict,* Chuck Colson tells a story of such an intimate friendship.

It was a quiet December evening on Ward C43, the oncology unit at Georgetown University Hospital. In Room 11, Jack Swigert, the man who had piloted the Apollo 13 lunar mission in 1970 and was now Congressman-elect from Colorado's 6th Congressional District, lay dying of cancer. With him, sitting in the spot he occupied almost every night since Swigert had been admitted, was Bill Armstrong, U.S. Senator from Colorado. But Bill Armstrong wasn't there as a powerful politician; as a deeply committed Christian, Armstrong was fulfilling his responsibility as a friend.

That night he leaned over the bed of his friend and said, "You're going to be all right, Jack. God loves you. I love you. You are surrounded by friends who are praying for you." Bill Armstrong pulled his chair closer to the bed and began reading Psalm 23. As time passed, he read Psalm 150. And then, Jack's ragged breathing stopped. Armstrong called for help, but as the nurse examined his friend, Bill knew there was nothing more he could do.

Politicians are busy people. Bill Armstrong was at that time the chairman of the Senate subcommittee handling Washington's hottest issue—Social Security. But he was not too busy to be at the bedside of a friend. Friends are available when we need them.[2]

Friends are often more honest than family members.

My mother listens to Christian radio throughout her day. In fact, where she lives, she can hear the program I appear on, *Back to the Bible,* three times a day on different stations. She listens to me three times each day even though it is the same broadcast. Why? Because she's my mother. If I was really having a lousy day and it showed up in my teaching on radio, I know one place I'd never hear an honest criticism—from Mom.

Now, not all families are like that, I know. Perhaps your family is always critical of you. But isn't that still the point. Our families are often biased—for us or against us. If you want an honest critique, you don't ask your family; you ask your friends.

Antisthenes, the cynic philosopher, once said, "There are only two people who will tell you the truth about yourself—an enemy who has lost his temper and a friend who loves you dearly." The Bible puts the issue this way: "Open rebuke is better than love carefully concealed. Faithful are the wounds of a friend" (Proverbs 27:5–6).

Leslie B. Flynn begins his delightful book *Great Church Fights* with a chapter entitled, "We Need Each Other," which contains this story: "Two porcupines in northern Canada huddled together to get warm, according to a forest folk tale. But their quills pricked each other and they moved apart. Before long they were shivering and they sidled close again. New scene; same ending. They needed each other, but they kept needling each other."[3] Even though your friends may needle you a little, they usually will be honest, direct, and straightforward. That's what friends are for.

Friends often influence us most.

Butch Cassidy and the Sundance Kid. Bonnie and Clyde. Thelma and Louise. Oscar Madison and Felix Unger. These are historical or cinematic characters who influenced each other. Unfortunately, that influence was not always positive. Friends wield a significant amount of influence. They shape our thinking. They mold our morality. That's why peer pressure is such a big deal. For better or worse, friends often determine our life's course.

There can be little argument, therefore, that friends should be chosen carefully. As Proverbs 13:20 says, "He who walks with wise men will be wise, but the companion of fools will be destroyed." We should always select friends who will help us up, not keep us down.

But just as bad friends have a bad influence on us, good friends have a good influence on us. A recent study by researchers at Ohio State University Medical School revealed that fellowship with friends can improve your health. The researchers discovered that close friendships help to decrease stress and therefore boost the body's immune system.[4] If this is true physically, is there any reason to believe it would not be true spiritually as well? Godly friends can boost your spiritual immune system, helping you to fend off all kinds of "viruses."

Friends may become soulmates.

Friends come in all shapes and sizes. There are girlfriends, boyfriends, and "just" friends. Friends are multigenerational, multinational, and multiethnic. Friends come and go with the times. But often the person with the greatest impact on our life is our "soulmate." A soulmate is our best friend, our friend for life. This person sees things the way we do, thinks like we do, and may even say things at exactly the same time as we do.

Two examples from the Bible help us to understand this soulmate kind of friendship. The first example is David and Jonathan. In 1 Samuel, we read, "The soul of Jonathan was knit to the soul of David, and Jonathan loved him as his own soul" (18:1). It is ludicrous to think that their relationship was anything but heterosexual. Their souls, not their bodies, were knit together in love. But the friendship between David and Jonathan was so close that it surpassed their love for anyone else. When David needed advice, who do you think would have the greatest impact on his thinking? Joab? Michel? Samuel? No, it was Jonathan. They were soulmates.

The same was true for Paul and Timothy. The apostle said of Timothy, "I have no one like-minded, who will sincerely care for your state" (Philippians 2:20). The word he used was *isopsuchos,* which means "of equal soul." It comes from two Greek words, *isos* meaning equal and *psuche* meaning the seat of our feelings and desires. Paul and Timothy saw things alike. They had similar passions. They impacted the thinking and behavior of each other.

When friends are family

Earlier I said that friends often influence us more than family members. That's true. But let's not neglect the fact that sometimes our siblings, parents, aunts or uncles, or cousins become our good friends. You may not have family members who can help you spiritually because they do not share your beliefs. But if there are members of your immediate or extended family who are also members of your spiritual family, you are fortunate indeed. These people often become our friends, our encouragers, our cheerleaders.

Throughout this book I refer to my family—my wife and children, my father and mother, and others. That's because I have been blessed by God with a wonderfully supportive family. They have played a huge role in shaping my spiritual life because they are more than family to me. They have been my friends as well. My older brother, Jerry, is a pastor in Virginia. He is twenty-one months older than I am, and I have always looked up to him. We have another brother, Ron, who is twelve years younger than me. The three of us have grown much closer as adults than we were as kids. That's because we began to appreciate each other more as friends, not just family. Since Ron began first grade the year I went off to college, I really didn't get to know him until he was an adult. Now I don't know how I got along without him all those years. My parents and my brothers weren't just inspirations to me as family; they were, and are, extremely influential to my spiritual life.

Another family member who has been a remarkable friend is my wife, Linda. She is my true soulmate, who keeps me on track spiritually. Linda has taught me the joy of simplicity, of taking things one day at a time, of being patient with little hands covered with peanut butter and jelly. I see it as my role as husband to help her grow spiritually, but she has taught me more than she can know about spiritual things.

Once, while flying across the Atlantic Ocean returning from a speaking tour in Europe, I looked over at Linda, who was sound asleep with her head on a pillow against the plane's window. As I looked at her, I realized how much less stressful her life would be if she had never met me, and I thanked the Lord for a godly wife who was my best friend. I took out a piece of paper from my Bible and jotted down these words: "There is a friend who's dear to me, as dear to me as life; but I choose not to call her friend, I choose to call her wife."

What a blessing it is when your family and your friends are the same people. You get the benefits that friends bring in shaping your spiritual life, and you get the benefits of family as well. It's a double blessing.

The sequoia trees of California tower as much as three hundred feet above the ground. But surprisingly, these giants have an unusually shallow root system that reaches out in all directions to capture the moisture in the ground. Seldom will you find a redwood standing alone because the high winds would uproot it. That's why they grow in clusters. Their intertwining roots provide support for one another against the storms. That's what friends do, too.

ENLIST THE HELP OF MENTORS

The other day Linda and I were looking through some old photographs. Among the pictures were some official-looking documents—they were mementos of our childhood.

One of those documents was a Vacation Bible School certificate. It was dated June 21, 1953, and said, "This certificate is awarded to Linda Piper for regular attendance and faithful work in the primary department of Vacation Bible School." It was signed, "Rev. Frank Kroll, Pastor" and "Mrs. Betty Kroll, Teacher." Linda couldn't have known it then, but the two people who signed her VBS certificate would years later become her in-laws.

The relationship between older and younger people can be antagonistic and uncaring, or it can be sympathetic and nurturing. When it's a mentoring relationship, it's a beautiful thing.

A mentor is more than a friend. Friends interact with your life by joining you at ball games, sitting with you in church, attending your son's birthday party, and sending you a Christmas card. There is an equal relationship in friendship. Each gives, each receives. Being a mentor, however, is more. A mentor is someone farther down the road than you, someone who is going where you want to go, and who is willing to give you some light to help you get there.

Putting experience to work

In Greek mythology, Mentor was the aged advisor and friend of Odysseus. When Odysseus went off to fight the Trojan war, he entrusted Mentor with the education of his son, Telemachus. Taking our cue from the origin of the word, a mentor is a trusted counselor or guide. Being a mentor is like being a tutor or coach, and that's a much more responsible relationship than a friend. A mentor usually is an older man or woman passing down wisdom and guidance to someone of the same gender, but that need not always be the case. Mentors can be found in families, church, education, and business.

In her book *Mentors and Proteges,* Linda Phillips-Jones gives numerous examples of seasoned career women who were eager to train and encourage younger, less experienced women. Specifically, she tells of Katherine S. White, the late fiction editor of *The New Yorker,* who was known as a woman ready to nurture young writers in their craft. Phillips-Jones says, "When White died, the magazine was deluged with letters that praised her and described the profound effect that her deep sense of caring had on people's lives."[5]

The Bible is filled with examples of mentors, people who deeply cared, cared enough to tutor in eternal values. Just think of Moses and Joshua, Naomi and Ruth, Paul and Timothy, Elizabeth and Mary, Elijah and Elisha, Barnabas and Mark, Abraham and Lot, Jesus and the disciples. In each case, someone farther down the road helped another person to gain maturity.

The key passage in the Bible that relates to mentoring is Titus 2:1–6. Take some time to read it. Most of what we need to know about mentoring can be learned from these verses. Consider the following.

Mentors don't suddenly appear with a big "M" on their chest. All you have to do to be a mentor is care enough to give whatever you have. Mentors aren't trained professionals who have been to mentoring school. Mentors don't have a Ph.D. in "mentorology." Mentors are mothers and dads; they are grandmothers and grandfathers; they are neighbors, bosses, even mothers-in-law.

A mentor is often a professional, but doesn't have to be. In Titus 2:1–6, Paul addresses older men and older women in general, not *skilled* older men or *educated* older women. Anyone can be a mentor. All you have to do to be a mentor is care enough to give whatever you have.

Mentoring need not be a formal arrangement.

Lots of people are part of small Bible studies, Sunday school classes, cell groups, or women's clubs. But while these venues may be the setting for teaching, they are not always best for mentoring. Often mentoring is done on the telephone, in the kitchen, on the road, or in the neighborhood café. Mentoring is lubricated with coffee and fed with a bagel. It often works best when it is not a formal arrangement or rigidly monitored. It is the casual but continual effort to make everything in our life meaningful to someone else God has brought into our life. A good mentor never really stops mentoring.

"I'm not sure about the advisability of going fishing with a man named 'Frank Drown'," Kurt said with a laugh. Kurt, a staff member with *Back to the Bible,* was part of a group of men from Lincoln, Nebraska, who was going on a fishing expedition to Canada. "But I've never met a man who knows so much about missions, or about the Lord."

Frank Drown, a veteran missionary who served with his wife in South America, now runs a fishing camp north of Thunder Bay, Ontario. Each week young missionaries come to Frank's camp for mentoring and relaxation, as do individuals from churches across the United States and Canada. Frank and his family and friends take them fishing and in the process talk with them about spiritual things, including missions.

"There's just something about getting someone out in a boat on a lake that gives you a perfect opportunity to talk about the Lord," Frank said. "Even if the fish aren't biting, there are significant things we can talk about—and we have an opportunity to model things like patience and long-suffering. After all, fishing is a lot like life—it has its share of frustrations."

Casual conversation is as successful a mentoring method as institutional instruction. Remember what the Lord told parents about passing on God's commandments to their children: "You shall teach them diligently to your children [that's teaching], and shall talk of them when you sit in your house, when you walk by the way, when you lie down, and when you rise up" (Deuteronomy 6:7). That's mentoring!

Mentoring is about successful living, not theological dogma. The older women in the New Testament were to mentor the younger in everyday, practical things. The same is true today. Older women help their younger counterparts with things like how to develop a healthy, loving marriage; how to be discreet in what you talk about on the phone with a girlfriend or over the back fence with a neighbor; how to make a house into a home that the family enjoys; and how to be patient with the children after a nasty accident involving chocolate syrup and white carpet.

These are not theological lessons; they are the stuff of life. Mentoring is not about the big ideas as much as it is about the little lessons that those with experience pass on to novices. Mentors know their task is to "fill in the details." They are not instructors of systematic theology, but practitioners of "show-me" theology. Mentoring is just one successful life showing another life how to be successful.

Don't think that you have to limit yourself to mentoring—or being mentored—by one person. Everybody knows that Paul mentored Timothy, but he also mentored Titus (2 Corinthians 8:23), Tychicus (Colossians 4:7), Silas (Acts 15:40), and Sosthenes (1 Corinthians 1:1). Moses mentored Joshua, but he also mentored Aaron and Caleb. Naomi mentored Ruth, but she also mentored Orpah to a lesser degree (Ruth 1:4). Not all of Mark's mentoring was from Barnabas (Acts 15:39). Apparently, he was also mentored by Peter who may have provided first-hand information for Mark's gospel and by Paul himself (2 Timothy 4:11).

If you enlist the help of only one mentor, you may not have tapped into the wisdom and expertise God has placed around you. Paul Griffis was a mentor to me, but so were M. L. Lowe, William Lane, John L. Benson, and Roger Nicole. Some of my Sunday school teachers when I was a boy were mentors to me as well, people like Lawrence Francis and Archie Nagel. To be successful in your Christian life, find a mentor. To be really successful, find more than one.

ENLIST THE HELP OF YOUR PASTOR

Pastors are special people. I know; I've been surrounded by them. I grew up in a pastor's home. My father pastored the same church for thirty-three years. My first ministry after graduation from seminary was pastoring a church in Massachusetts. How patient those people were as I made so many mistakes. And now, even though I'm involved in a teaching and writing ministry, I am still surrounded by pastors. I've mentioned that my older brother is a pastor, but I haven't mentioned that my only son is as well. The church in which I am a member has a staff of pastors, each charged with specific duties. Pastors are a part of my life. I understand them. I am one of them. I appreciate them.

If you want superior help in living your Christian life, enlist the help of your pastor. My former pastors—people like Floyd Ellis, Donald George, and Curt Lehman—had a profound impact on my ministry. There's nobody like a pastor to guide you in seeing things more clearly.

Pastor as shepherd

It's probably been a long time, if ever, since you've been on a sheep farm or even seen a sheep up close and personal. The image of sheep and shepherds in the Bible comes right out of the ancient Near East, but it is timeless, understandable, helpful even today. Shepherds guide their sheep, gently nudging them when they don't always want to follow. They lead their sheep (Psalm 80:1), provide for the needs of the sheep (Psalm 23:1), keep the sheep from trouble (Zechariah 10:2), and rescue them when they are in danger (Amos 3:12). Shepherds protect their sheep (John 10:11), because they are the legitimate caretaker of the sheep (John 10:2). They are the key to keeping the flock together (Matthew 26:31). They exert authority over the flock (Ezekiel 37:24); they are intimately aware of the needs of their sheep (John 10:14); they feed the flock (Isaiah 40:11), and teach them what the sheep need to know to be successful (Mark 6:34).

Look to your pastor for leadership, to provide for your spiritual needs, to keep you from trouble, and rescue you when you are sinking spiritually. When you don't know where to turn, when the information you have received and the advice you have been given is conflicting, look to the shepherd in your life.

Pastor as counselor

Not only is the pastor your caregiver and guide, he is also the spiritual counselor in your life. He's the one divinely ordained to give you counsel from God's Word. Paul told Timothy the pastor would not only preach the Word, he would also convince his people of the truth. Sometimes he may have to rebuke his people for straying from the truth, but the pastor would always encourage them through the teaching of the Word (2 Timothy 4:2). It's a heavenly combination: God's ordained man, using God's inspired Word, to guide God's bewildered people.

Your pastor can help you with a wide variety of needs. He is not there for you just when your marriage is falling apart. Pastoral counsel is not just for that horrible day when you lose your dearest one on earth. Your pastor is there to provide biblical counsel on choosing a mate or choosing a vocation, identifying mission opportunities or identifying your spiritual gifts, deciding between competing universities or competing responsibilities, handling personal temptation or handling personal finances, caring for your teens or caring for your aging parents. Your pastor is not an expert in all things, and you shouldn't expect him to be. But when you need counsel for direction in your life, you've got a good friend in your pastor.

Paul taught the Ephesians that Christ gave His church various officers to ensure that the church would be successful. One of those officers is the pastor-teacher (4:11). Jesus selected and gifted people in the church "for the equipping of the saints for the work of the ministry" (4:12). Your pastor has been placed by Jesus Christ in the church not only to give you advice but to equip you in following that advice. He counsels you for the work of the ministry not just for your personal benefit. Your pastor is your equipper, the enabler who teaches you the Word and encourages you in the skills and gifts necessary to serve the Lord.

Pastor as wise man

In the olden days of Israel, three classes of people ministered to God's people. The priest ministered at the altar, offering sacrifices to God on behalf of the people (Exodus 30:30). The prophet had the opposite ministry. He received messages from God and communicated them to the people on behalf of God (1 Samuel 3:20). And the wise man or sage was not a prophet or a priest, but one divinely endowed to give practical advice (1 Chronicles 27:32). Jeremiah 18:18 lists all three in one breath: "Then they said, 'Come and let us devise plans against Jeremiah; for the law shall not perish from the priest, nor counsel from the wise, nor the word from the prophet."

Since the days of the early church until now, God has called and gifted individuals to function in all three of these roles. Pastors are not only called to preach, counsel, and administer; they are called to be men of wisdom. They have tapped into the wisdom that comes through God's Word, the "depth of the riches both of the wisdom and knowledge of God" (Romans 11:33).

I have a pastor friend, Don, who told me about a situation that required all of his wisdom. A couple in his church, Carl and Carrie, were on the brink of divorce. Years earlier, Carl had lost interest in her and spent all his time "hanging out" with the guys he worked with. She in turn cultivated her own set of friends, and before they knew it, both were unfaithful. Their anger at each other over the breakdown of the marriage and the violation of the vows led them to insist that "it was over and there was no hope for saving it." The only reason Carl and Carrie came to see the pastor was because her parents begged that they give it one last try.

When they came to see Don, they sat on opposite sides of his office. About halfway through the session, Pastor Don asked, "Carl, you claim to be a Christian, and you know Scripture tells husbands to love their wives—"

"I don't think of her as a wife anymore, Pastor," Carl said, interrupting. "She means no more to me than the neighbor down the street."

Don countered, "Well, Scripture says we are to love our neighbor as ourselves."

"I know, Pastor," Carl replied, "but she's worse than a neighbor. She's more like an enemy."

"Well," Don continued, "Scripture says, 'Love your enemies.' Carl, you're still required to love her."

Frowning and shaking his head, Carl said, "But I'd be a hypocrite, Pastor. I have no feelings for her whatever."

Praying for wisdom, Pastor Don responded, "Well, Carl, why don't you try for a week to treat her as though you did love her. I know what you're going to say—you'd only be *acting* like you love her. But I think if you act as if you love her and if she acts like she loves you, the feelings might follow."

The next week Carl and Carrie walked into Don's office and the hostility level, while not totally dissipated, was significantly lower. As they talked with Pastor Don, both agreed that their choice to treat each other with love and respect had made a difference. While their problems certainly didn't disappear in a few sessions, ultimately they reconciled and rebuilt their marriage.

When you need help in understanding spiritual things, turn to your pastor. He is a man of the Word, and he is a man of wisdom—the kind of wisdom you need if you want to be successful in living the Christian life. Your pastor can sniff out bad advice the way a restaurant guide can sniff out bad food. When you want medical advice, you know where to go. When you want spiritual advice, don't fail to find it where God has deposited it.

ENLIST THE HELP OF THE HOLY SPIRIT

We now come to help with a capital H. If you want to be successful in living the Christian life, you'll find no greater help than the Holy Spirit. The Spirit of God not only brings you to the Savior, He also helps you throughout your Christian life (John 14:16–17).

The Christian life demands far more from us than our human resources can provide. It doesn't take us very long to learn that. But, by means of our divine Helper, we can anticipate success. He stands ready to live through us, to empower us, to energize us, to help us to be and to do all that God requires of us. When we enlist the superior help of the Holy Spirit, how does He make us successful? Here are some ways.

He prays for us (Romans 8:26–27).

Have you ever needed to pray but didn't know what to say? Your emotions were running wild, but your mind wasn't keeping up. You just couldn't find the words to express what your heart was telling you. Suppose you found yourself in an impossible situation. Your mother was critically ill and on life support. The doctors had pronounced her "brain dead." They want to know if you want her to remain on life support. The decision is yours and yours alone. What will you decide? You need help. You need to pray, but your mind is so scrambled you don't know how.

When your chances of success seem slim, and your prayers are stymied by desperation, it's good to experience the praying ministry of the Holy Spirit. The Spirit of God prays for you with inaudible, inexpressible sighs, and the Father hears His Spirit even when we cannot pray to Him. The Father knows the mind of the Holy Spirit, who always prays according to the divine will (v. 27), and when you pray in God's will, you always pray with success.

That's the kind of praying aid we all need. Ask for the Spirit's help when you pray. Ask Him to make you successful in living the Christian life. Ask Him to pray for you, about you, with you.

He teaches us (1 John 2:27).

The Holy Spirit gives the Christian an understanding of divine truth as no one else can (John 14:26; 1 Corinthians 2:11–12). He also helps us to distinguish between truth and error (1 John 4:1–6). We need never fall to the subtlety of false teachers who frequent our door if we are consistently in the Word and are being taught by the Spirit. God's people are not abandoned to the fallibility of human teachers. We can check everything we hear against what the Spirit of God teaches us from His Word. In fact, apart from the Spirit's teaching ministry in our lives, it is impossible for any of us to understand fully the Word of God (1 Corinthians 2:11–12, 14; 2 Corinthians 4:3–4).

Years ago, I met a young man named Francis. He was a black African, and I first saw him standing in the doorway of an Italian youth hostel. I had stayed there the night before with a group of college students. I noticed several of my students had engaged him in conversation, and they brought him to me with his questions. To the best of my ability, I answered his questions about why there was so much hate in the world, why racism was so rampant, and why there seemed to be no hope. I have learned that when people ask these kinds of questions it is because they have a deeper need, and I always turn them to Jesus Christ and the Bible for answers.

After forty minutes of telling Francis about God's love for him and Christ's sacrifice for him, the tears started streaming down his cheeks. Francis was gloriously saved. It was written all over his face. I gave him a Bible and my address and told him to begin reading. When we parted, I didn't really expect to hear from him again.

Then, about two months later, I received a letter from Francis. He had been studying his Bible alone and had two pages of questions for me to answer. Conscientiously, I answered each question and encouraged him to keep on studying his Bible. About six weeks later, another letter arrived with several more pages of questions. Again I answered. Francis had no teacher, no library, no mentor close by to help him grow. He studied alone, and read the Bible by himself. The Holy Spirit was his guide. And still, in his third letter he said, "I have encountered people who say they are the witnesses of Jehovah, but what they teach is wrong. It's not what I have learned from my Bible." Francis is proof that a person can grow by himself or herself with the help of the Holy Spirit.

Try it for yourself. Sit down to read your Bible. Take a pen and paper, or sit before your computer ready to make notes. Then ask the Spirit of God to show you some glorious insight you may never have seen before, even if you have read the passage a hundred times. Make David's prayer your prayer: "Open my eyes, that I may see wondrous things from Your law" (Psalm 119:18). That's how you get superior help.

He guides us (Romans 8:14).

But the Holy Spirit's work is not done when we have dug for new insights from God's Word. Paul informed his fellow Christians in ancient Rome, "For as many as are led by the Spirit of God, these are sons of God" (Romans 8:14). The verb "led" probably has as much to do with management as it does with showing the way. If you look to God's Spirit for direction, He will both reveal God's will to you and then manage your steps to guide you in God's way (Acts 16:6–10).

How does the Holy Spirit guide us? Several ways; let's think about three of the most obvious.

First, He uses the Scriptures. David prayed, "Show me Your ways, O LORD; teach me Your paths. Lead me in Your truth and teach me, for You are the God of my salvation; on You I wait all the day" (Psalm 25:4–5). If that's your prayer, too, when you read God's Word, your prayers are answered. The precepts and principles found there often clearly indicate God's will for us (Psalm 119:11, 105; 1 Peter 2:15). The Bible is the primary way God directs us.

Second, He leads us by inward impressions or urges (Isaiah 30:21; Luke 2:27). We simply know God wants us to do something. How do we know? The Spirit confirms with our spirit that it's the right thing to do. Before we follow these urges, however, we must be certain of their source. A lot of competing voices come to us. We must test our impressions against what the Bible clearly teaches and seek their confirmation by prayer.

In his book *Flying Closer to the Flame,* Chuck Swindoll proposes two practical suggestions about following our inner impressions. First, when you are not sure that something is from the Spirit, tread softly. And second, when you are confident that it's of God, stand firm, even against other people's doubts.[6]

Finally, the Holy Spirit guides us through our circumstances (Acts 16:6–12; Galatians 4:13 with Acts 13:14). God providentially uses the circumstances of our lives to reveal His will to us. Paul told his friends at Philippi, "But I want you to know, brethren, that the things which happened to me have actually turned out for the furtherance of the gospel" (Philippians 1:12). If you give yourself to the Holy Spirit's leadership, you'll receive His guidance (Proverbs 3:5–6).

He sanctifies us (2 Corinthians 3:18).

Spiritual success requires holding our lives to the right standard. The Holy Spirit is constantly making us more like Christ, God's perfect standard, and thereby He is constantly making us more successful in living the Christian life. He does this by sanctifying us. To be sanctified means to be set apart to God for His use. This occurs positionally when we are saved (1 Corinthians 1:2; 6:11), but it also occurs practically throughout our Christian life. To be like our holy God, which is a measure of success in itself, we must be holy in our daily behavior (1 Peter 1:15–16), and that's not easy. In fact, it's next to impossible. But that's where the Holy Spirit helps us. Enlisting His help in sanctifying us is one of the secrets of success in living the Christian life.

And how do we experience this sanctification? We must separate ourselves from every attitude and every pattern of behavior that is unlike Jesus and give ourselves to those attitudes and patterns of behavior that clearly align us with Him (Colossians 3:8–14). The Holy Spirit will accomplish this in your life as you respond to His prompting, instruction, and discipline (John 17:17; 15:3; Hebrews 12:10).

He fills us (Ephesians 5:18).

To be filled with the Holy Spirit doesn't mean we progressively receive more of Him. Since the Holy Spirit is a person, and you can't have a piece of a person, He wholly resides in us from the moment of our salvation. To be filled with the Holy Spirit means to be under His control. We are not under His control in the absolute sense. That would mean that we are passive and mindlessly controlled by Him. But when we are under the Spirit's control in a relative sense, we cooperate with Him by doing what He enables us to do while depending on Him to do for us what we are not able (Acts 2:4; 4:8, 31). This allows Him both to energize us for success and to do through us all that He desires to make us successful.

He gifts us (1 Corinthians 12:1–31).

There is a fundamental difference between spiritual gifts and native abilities. We are born with native abilities; spiritual gifts only come when we are born again. Native abilities belong to our human nature. They are capable of training and development, like singing or speaking. They may be used in service to the Lord if we yield them to Him. Some native abilities, like teaching and leadership, are similar to certain spiritual gifts, but they are not identical.

To ensure our spiritual success, however, the Holy Spirit gives us special gifts to augment our native abilities. As Elizabeth Barrett Browning said, "God's gifts put men's best dreams to shame." Spiritual gifts are really special activities the Holy Spirit does through us. The word *gifts* (1 Corinthians 12:4; Romans 12:6) means "grace-gifts." Since spiritual gifts are distributed according to the Holy Spirit's sovereign will (1 Corinthians 12:11), we cannot arbitrarily select a gift. We can't say, "I'll take that one." Spiritual gifts are not for self-edification; they are for our ministry to others in building the church (Ephesians 4:7–16). One of the best ways to be successful as a Christian is to make others successful. Spiritual gifts help us do that.

He renews us (Romans 12:1–2).

Imagine this scenario. Your business tycoon uncle dies and leaves you everything. Among your new possessions is his computer. You boot it up to see what he had on his hard drive. You are shocked. There is evidence of shady business deals, critical letters to his pastor, lists of competitors and their weaknesses, even some love letters to his partner's wife. There's no arguing with what's on the screen—it's despicable stuff.

But now the computer is under new ownership—your ownership. Those old files have to be removed, discarded, never to return. You go in and delete them one at a time. In their place you create new files. You input new and vital information for your life and future. The old is gone, the new has come to stay.

That's what the Spirit of God does when He renews your mind. Remember Paul's words to the Christians at Rome? "Do not be conformed to this world, but be transformed by the renewing of your mind" (Romans 12:2). Here Paul chose the Greek word *anakainosis*, meaning to have a new form or take on a new substance. When we enlist the Holy Spirit's aid, He constantly helps us to delete the old files from our mind and to save the new files created from our time in God's Word.

That's exactly what happened to Brad Scott. As a young man, his life was void of meaning. Searching for satisfaction he discovered the occult writings of Edgar Cayce, Jess Stearn, Alice Bailey, and others. They taught Brad that he could find meaning within himself by experiencing the Inner Truth. He believed he could discover the Secret of the Ages and use his Powers of Mind to overcome his insecurities. Buoyed by these teachings, he was drawn to Eastern mysticism and studied under a swami of the Ramakrishna Order for seven years.

But Brad's emptiness persisted. After all his striving to be pure, he realized that he had achieved nothing. "My torment finally ended a few days before Christmas in 1978. As eclectic yogis do in that season, I was reading the New Testament. In anguish, conscious of my own sinfulness, I paused over the story of the sinful woman who bathed Jesus' feet in her tears (Luke 7:36–50). As I contemplated the mercy Jesus showed here, I was suddenly struck by my own overwhelming need for forgiveness." Brad trusted Jesus Christ as Savior, and immediately the Holy Spirit of God began to reprogram his mind, deleting old things and saving new ones. "Jesus Christ, I discovered, is the secret of the ages: 'the mystery of God...in whom are hidden all the treasures of wisdom and knowledge' (Colossians 2:2–3)."[7]

You can successfully get rid of your old haunts, your old thought patterns, your old mind. And you can replace all the old with what's new in Christ Jesus. But if you want to do this successfully, enlist the help of the Holy Spirit. Give Him control to the keyboard of your mind, and let Him start deleting those files you should have ditched long ago.

SUCCESS SURVEY #4

1. *Do you feel like your spiritual growth is a solo project?* Up to this point, has it been something you've tried to accomplish by yourself? God has placed friends in each of our lives for our benefit. Do you have friends who can help you climb spiritual mountains? Enlist them. Do you have friends who can help you plummet into the depths of spiritual quicksand? Avoid them.

2. *If you were asked to picture the face of your mentor, who would come to your mind's eye? Anyone?* Have you had the benefit of a spiritual mentor, someone to show you the ropes as a Christian? If not, such mentors are readily available. Find one. Where will you look? Look for a spiritual mentor in your church, your small group, among your friends, even in your family? Is it possible God's mentor for your life has been near to you, and you've missed him or her?

3. *How well do you know your pastor?* Is he someone you can confide in? How do you know? Have you tried? Pastors are God's gift to His church, and if you are a member of a local church, your pastor is God's gift to you. The next time you need spiritual direction, an answer to a question you've been grappling with, or just someone to talk to, try your pastor. Do you think he's too busy? Listen, Christ gave His life for you. You are important to God. No pastor should be too busy to help one for whom Christ died. You won't know until you ask. Perhaps someone else on the church staff can help you, but in order to grow spiritually, enlist this help.

4. *Does the Holy Spirit seem like some divine phantom to you?* Is He real in your life? Do you feel His presence? Is there evidence of His presence? When you don't know how to pray, do you enlist His help? God has promised it; take advantage of it. And what about when you're confused over a spiritual issue or a thorny doctrinal problem? Who are you going to turn to? God's Holy Spirit is even closer to you than friends, mentors, and pastors. To be spiritually successful, rely on His help. He's just a prayer away.

5. *Whose help are you getting?* If you really want to be successful, you have to become a different person. Even if you gain the whole world, you are the loser if you are not a spiritual success as a Christian. Are you ready to make the commitment? Are you ready to see what it takes and who it takes to help you grow to spiritual maturity. You can be an impact player for God, but you can't get there alone. Are you willing to ask God for some help? Getting the right help makes all the difference in the world.

SPIRITUAL SECRET #5

LEARN TO MANAGE TEMPTATION

Temptation: the fiend at my elbow.
WILLIAM SHAKESPEARE

"Watch and pray, lest you enter into temptation."
MARK 14:38

———❦❦❦———

N othing robs us of spiritual success so devastatingly as yielding to temptation.[1] It may be the temptation of money, lust, power, position, sex, fame, perpetual youth, greed, or a hundred other things. Whatever it is, it always seems to be there. While opportunity knocks but once, temptation seems to be constantly banging on our door.

There's that once-in-a-lifetime deal that will make you a lot of money in a hurry but is as shady as a Banyan tree in the rain forest. There's the lady next door who always seems to be sunbathing when you're cutting the grass. There's the preapproved credit card application that arrives in your mail, even though you have already maxed out three other cards. There's the guy at the office who seems to be paying more attention to you than he should, and you kind of like it. Temptations come in all shapes and sizes, through all hours of the day or night. And the Christian is no less susceptible than anyone else.

When *Leadership* magazine commissioned a poll of a thousand pastors concerning temptation, 12 percent of them admitted that they had committed adultery while in the ministry. And 23 percent said they did something they considered sexually inappropriate while serving as a pastor.[2] *Christianity Today* magazine surveyed a thousand of its subscribers (not pastors) and discovered that 23 percent admitted to committing adultery and 45 percent admitted to doing something they deemed sexually inappropriate.[3]

Statistics may give us a snapshot of the number of people succumbing to temptation, but it's the real-life stories, the flesh-and-blood accounts, that impact us the most. We hear about a respected couple from church who are getting a divorce after twenty-five years of marriage—apparently the husband found someone younger and more attractive. We learn about a neighbor who is losing his house and filing for bankruptcy—his gambling problem finally caught up with him. We discover a coworker has been abruptly dismissed for downloading pornographic material from his computer on work time. How do these things happen?

Of course, temptation itself is not the problem; resisting it is the problem. British writer Oscar Wilde said, "I can resist anything except temptation." To be sure, resisting temptation is not easy, but the only way to be a spiritual success is to manage the temptations that confront us. It can be done, but it can't be done alone, and it can't be done without a plan.

Dave was a friend of mine. I've lost track of him now, but I used to work closely with him years ago when I was pursuing graduate education. Few people had the skills on the basketball court that Dave had. Relatively short by basketball standards (six foot two) he could dribble between his legs or behind his back, he was a master at the outlet pass, and he could dunk the ball with either hand. After playing basketball successfully at the high school and college levels, he dreamed of a professional career, but he knew his height would make that only a fantasy. So he entered the business world instead.

Dave had committed his life to Christ as a young man, but he always seemed to have a weakness for the opposite sex. Although married with two small children, he began to find himself attracted to Cindy, a lady who worked in his office. They began sharing meals together in the lunchroom each day. Dave was active in his church, though much of his life was a sham. Nobody at church knew it, but his spiritual life was in the pits. It wasn't long before he was involved in a full-blown affair with Cindy, one which cost him his job, his position in the church, and his family. What a tragedy! Someone so bright and talented, with a future full of promise, and he threw it all away. Why? Because he couldn't—or rather wouldn't—resist temptation.

In the pages that follow, we will explore five simple steps to manage temptation. Unfortunately, the simpler the steps, the more apt we are to overlook them. That's what Dave did. I pray these steps will be like the electronic tags attached to clothing in department stores. They are there to detect shoplifters and prevent theft. If the device is tampered with in any way, or if someone tries to steal something from the store, a loud alarm goes off, and the thief is stopped in his tracks. As we struggle to achieve spiritual success, may we hear the alarm ringing in our head every time we are tempted.

TO RESIST TEMPTATION, PREPARE FOR IT

There is no reason for a Christian to be surprised when temptation comes. We have the history of humankind, from Adam and Eve onward, that shows how Satan has worked in the past. With the success he has had, why would he want to change tactics? In fact, you probably have a history of dealing with the devil personally. You've done battle with him before. Therefore, to be spiritually successful, be like the Boy Scouts—always prepared. If Satan catches you off guard, if he spots you with your defenses down, he knows half the battle is won.

So how can you prepare for the temptations that are just around the bend? What can you do right now to prepare for the temptations you may face on your date tonight? Well, don't despair. The Bible will help you. Here are some things you can do to prepare for temptation.

Identify your personal weaknesses.

We all have them. Call them foibles. Call them chinks in our spiritual armor. Call them defects, weaknesses, or blind spots. Call them whatever you want, but they are the areas of life where we are most susceptible to attack by Satan. He has an uncanny way of finding them. Just when we think they are hidden, like a smart bomb, his arrows find their way into our lives.

Satan's arrow found its way to Moses' weakness—anger—so that when he yielded to temptation the result was murder (Exodus 2). His arrow found Elijah's weakness—depression—and when he yielded to temptation, he suffered his greatest defeat on the heels of his greatest victory (1 Kings 19). The arrow of Satan found its way to Jacob's weakness—deception—and the result was a brother out to kill him (Genesis 27). The devil's arrow found its way to Peter's weakness—volatility—so that when he yielded to temptation it meant a public denial of his Lord (Matthew 26). The list goes on and on.

Remember the Peter problem.

Can you identify those areas of life where you are most vulnerable to Satan's attack? Most of us can. They are the areas we don't want to talk about. Sometimes we even deny we have a problem in these areas.

When Jesus informed His disciples that they would all forsake Him and scatter that very night, self-confident Peter replied, "Even if all are made to stumble because of You, I will never be made to stumble" (Matthew 26:33). Big mistake. Peter thought he was incapable of denying the Lord. He had been such a resolute comrade. But Peter was blind to his personal weaknesses. That seems to be a problem for many of us. Satan saw something that Peter didn't. He knew Peter's self-confidence was the chink in his armor. Peter had been volatile before. He should have seen it coming, but he didn't. So Satan immediately went to work, and within hours Peter fell to temptation and denied his Lord.

It's always easy to identify areas of personal weakness in others. Paul's ability to size up his understudy, Timothy, is a good example. The apostle knew that Timothy was timid, so he advised, "God has not given us a spirit of fear, but of power and of love and of a sound mind" (2 Timothy 1:7). He knew Timothy's youth would be filled with the usual temptations of his age, so he counseled, "Flee also youthful lusts" (2 Timothy 2:22). Paul knew, too, that Timothy's youthfulness may have allowed him to be pushed around by those who were older, so the apostle said, "Let no one despise your youth" (1 Timothy 4:12). All the areas of personal weakness that may have been hidden to Timothy were blatantly obvious to Paul.

What is more difficult, however, is sizing up our own areas of personal weakness. It was like that with my old buddy, Dave. He would often make comments about the women he knew, not saying bad things, but making observations that would have been better left unsaid. He'd watch a woman walking in front of us on the street and would say, "Those sure are good walkin'-away jeans." What Dave didn't understand was how much his mind thought such things and how often his mouth followed. He just didn't believe sex was a personal weakness for him.

Until we identify our weaknesses, we cannot deal with them.

Prepare a defense.

Maybe that's how you can best prepare to defend against temptation. Ask someone you trust to help you identify your weaknesses and deal with them. If you are married and both your spouse and you are Christians, who would know the chinks in your spiritual armor better than your husband or wife? Help each other prepare a defense against temptation.

This isn't harping on each other's deficiencies. This is not being critical of one another. This is identifying areas you see Satan needling your spouse so you can help him or her muster a defense. Strengthen these areas of personal weakness together. It's a great way to grow closer in the Lord, together.

Ladies, if you have a big sister in the Lord, ask her to share with you what she sees as possible areas where Satan may gain a foothold in your life. And then listen to her when she tells you how she has been able to defend against similar temptations. Paul encouraged the older women to help the younger in areas like being gossips and busybodies (1 Timothy 5:13).

Carla worked in a large office and was very active in her church, particularly in the music ministry. Yet she struggled with frustrations in her marriage relationship, and occasionally found herself tempted to look to other men to meet the emotional needs her husband, Tim, couldn't seem to meet.

"I very nearly wound up having an affair," she said. "At least until I met Connie."

Twenty years older than Carla and the wife of a former pastor, Connie took Carla under her wing. The two met together, studied the Word, and prayed. As Connie mentored Carla, the younger woman began to share her frustrations.

"She really helped me in relating to Tim," Carla said. "She helped me see where I was failing and seriously warned me about even harboring the idea of getting my needs met somewhere else. She's really helped stabilize me in the Lord."

Connie was more than a friend to Carla. She was a godsend. She mentored Carla and molded her into a loving and responsive wife. There are thousands of Carlas who need someone just like Connie. Maybe that's a ministry God has prepared for you. If you need a big sister, find a Connie. If you are a spiritually mature big sister, look for a Carla. You can be God's gift to each other.

Men, if you pray with brothers in the faith, hold each other accountable to shut the devil's foot in the door. As with women, older men were encouraged by Paul to mentor younger men in areas where they were most likely to be tempted to sin, such as self-control and integrity (Titus 2:6–7). Building defenses together not only thwarts the designs of Satan, but it also strengthens bonds between people.

I met Gary Purdy during a conference I spoke at in Bermuda last year. His wife had just died, and we held several tender conversations about it. In the process I learned about his son, Gary Jr., who is a missionary in Germany. He attributes his spiritual growth and success to his father.

Recently Gary Jr. said, "In a lot of ways, Dad's been like a big brother in the Lord. I don't think anybody's been more help to me spiritually. He's motivated me to study the Word, to seek God's will for my life, and to develop a heart for reaching lost people with the gospel. Not only that, he's *lived* his faith."

Christian parents can be invaluable in assessing your personal spiritual weaknesses. Having spent decades in the home together, parents can help their children identify the places where Satan's arrows are apt to land—places like greed, bitterness, selfishness, shyness, aggressiveness, self-confidence, defensiveness, self-pity, or jealousy. But parents, don't stop there. Help your children build defenses. Fathers have a special responsibility to help their sons overcome the temptation toward adultery. Read the father's counsel to his son in Proverbs 6:20–35.[4]

Preparing a defense is not like pulling the zipper up on a sleeping bag after you've crawled inside. We cannot fend off temptation by creating a cocoon around ourselves. We must figure out how to live in a tempting world—but in such a way that we live above the temptation. Let others help you identify your areas of weakness and prepare a defense against them. The only one who won't benefit from this strategy is Satan.

Tap God's resources.

The Bible is filled with advice on how to defend against the devil. That's why those who are more familiar with their Bibles are usually more successful in managing temptation. They tap God's resources.

The advice of God's Word ranges from the simple to the sublime, from the practical to the profound. For example, sublime and profound advice in getting ready for the war is found in Paul's words, "Put on the whole armor of God, that you may be able to stand against the wiles of the devil" (Ephesians 6:11). If you take seriously the whole armor of God and follow Paul's instructions for its use, you can take Satan on head to head. If you don't, you better get behind someone who has his armor on.

The simple and practical advice in getting ready to do battle with Satan is seen in many of Job's insightful resolves. "I have made a covenant with my eyes; why then should I look upon a young woman?" (Job 31:1). Even at his age, Job knew the temptation to lust was real. He knew it was his personal weakness, so he planned a defense. Job never fell to that temptation because he was ready for it.

Unlike Job, my friend Dave forgot to make a covenant with his eyes. In fact, his eyes were like a periscope, constantly scanning the horizon for anything or anyone who would fulfill his lust. Cindy wasn't the only gal at work Dave gave the once-over. She just happened to be the one who responded to Dave's incessant glances as they drew closer together. Often sin begins with sight, but it rarely stays there. It certainly didn't for Dave. Don't be afraid to admit your weaknesses and tap God's resources to provide you with strength.

Another of Job's simple resolves is found in Job 27:3–4: "As long as my breath is in me, and the breath of God in my nostrils, my lips will not speak wickedness, nor my tongue utter deceit." This kind of resolve is preparing in advance for the battle with Satan. What Job did that made him successful, you and I can do as well.

If you don't prepare yourself for the war, when the battle comes you'll fall like a rock the first time Satan slinks up to you with a brightly packaged temptation, even if you understand your enemy's battle plan. The secret to managing temptation is spiritual defense, and that's a lot like civil defense. Don't wait until the battle begins to get ready.

TO PREVENT TEMPTATION, AVOID IT

In a society filled with meaningless machismo, is it a sign of weakness to avoid temptation? Shouldn't the Christian face it head-on, even challenge it in the name and power of Jesus Christ? In his classic devotional *The Imitation of Christ,* Thomas a Kempis wrote: "We should not strive for a peace that is without temptation, or for a life that never feels adversity. Peace is not found by escaping temptations, but by being tried by them."[5] Did Thomas mean we should not try to avoid temptation but seek it out in order to be stronger? Of course not. That's the kind of reasoning that would justify hitting your thumb with a hammer to be able to better withstand future pain.

Those looking for the secret to spiritual success aren't looking for a fight with the devil. The spiritually astute don't challenge temptation. When it comes, they fight it, but wise men and women avoid temptation as much as possible. There is no honor in hunting down the devil and his haunts just to test your ability to manage temptation. That's foolishness, not faith.

Again, we can look to the Bible for help in avoiding temptation. The book of Proverbs is a virtual manual of advice on avoiding the snares of Satan. Much of it is a father writing to his son about how to manage temptation. Practical tips on controlling enticements abound (1:10; 2:12; 3:31; 5:1; 6:20–22; 7:1; 9:6; 10:1; 13:1). Many other books in the Bible also have stories about managing temptation (Genesis, Exodus, Joshua, Judges, Ruth, Samuel, Kings, Chronicles, Esther, Job, Psalms, Jeremiah, the Gospels, and Acts). In every case, the best advice on managing temptation is simply to avoid it in the first place.

Here are some insights from the Bible about avoiding temptation in order to achieve spiritual success.

Avoid tempting situations.

Some situations expose you to higher risk than others. If you want to live longer, avoid that bend in the road called "Dead Man's Curve." To maintain good health, cancel your vacation to the combination spa and leper colony. Skip the convention of those who have survived multiple lightning strikes. There are just some high-risk situations that you are advised to stay away from.

Dave and Cindy knew they were attracted to each other. Everyone at the office could see it in their eyes, and they could see it, too. Had either of them been wise enough to avoid each other, and especially the lunchroom when the other was there, they may not have given in to temptation. But they didn't do that. Each day at twelve thirty, they would come from different areas of the office, stop by the coffee machine in the lunchroom, and just "happen" to find each other at a corner table in the back of the room. You could set your watch by their punctuality.

Dave and Cindy weren't avoiding a tempting situation; they were caving in to it. In fact, they were seeking it out. There was a certain risk in their less-than-clandestine meetings, and they seemed to enjoy the danger of the risk. That's what destroyed them both. Dave and Cindy failed to avoid the most common tempting situation in sexual sin—the inappropriate meeting.

Let's face it, avoiding tempting situations means avoiding temptation. Unfortunately, like Dave and Cindy, most biblical examples of people avoiding tempting situations are those who didn't. David was the premier king of Israel. He was the man after God's own heart. But he was not above succumbing to temptation because he failed to avoid tempting situations. He provides an example for all of us.

David as a young leader

David was a handsome, young, brave, likable king. His early reign was one of complete success, both politically and spiritually. He became king in Hebron and seven and a half years later conquered Jerusalem, making it his political, social, and religious capital (2 Samuel 5:9). Immediately he demonstrated his military prowess and bravery by defeating his neighboring enemies—the Philistines (5:17–25), the Moabites (8:2), the Zobahites (8:3), the Syrians (8:5), and the Ammonites (10:1). Second Samuel 8:14 sums up David's military campaigns: "The LORD preserved David wherever he went."

Except for some smaller skirmishes (10:7), David always led his troops into battle. He was their king, their leader, their military strategist. He was the point man. His men loved him and would follow him anywhere. The only time David's leadership in battle failed is recorded in 2 Samuel 11. Verse 1 says, "In the spring of the year, at the time when kings go out to battle,...David sent Joab and his servants with him, and all Israel; and they destroyed the people of Ammon and besieged Rabbah. But David remained at Jerusalem."

David as a reluctant leader

This verse is no incidental historical comment. It describes David's failure both to lead, and more importantly for our study, to avoid tempting situations. From his palace rooftop, he looked down into the valley below him and saw a woman bathing. If you have been to Jerusalem and seen the ruins of David's city on the south side of the Old City, you can easily understand how David could look in on Bathsheba's bath time. Today, across the valley from David's city is the Arab village of Silwan, where the houses still are built in a stair-step fashion, one above the other, ascending the hill. David's palace would have been on the top of the hill and from the top, where David stood, every rooftop would have been visible. And it was on one of those rooftops that Bathsheba chose to bathe.

David's sin resulted from the usual progression of incremental steps. First, he saw Bathsheba bathing (v. 2). That was innocent enough, but it piqued his interest. Then he sent someone to find out who this woman was (v. 3). Already he had placed one foot on the slippery slope that leads to sin. Next, he yielded to temptation by sending for Bathsheba with the full intention of sleeping with her (v. 4). Finally, David involved others in his sin with Bathsheba, most notably Joab, his general, who became his accomplice in Uriah's murder (vv. 14–17).

David as an instructive leader

Could David have avoided giving in to his temptation? Absolutely. He was more than just in the wrong place at the wrong time. David failed to avoid a tempting situation, and more often than not, when we fail to avoid tempting situations we get caught by those situations.[6]

Proverbs 7 describes a young man who was trapped by yielding to a prostitute. Verses 7–9 say, "A young man devoid of understanding, passing along the street near her corner; and he took the path to her house." That sounds innocent enough, doesn't it? But failure even to avoid the vicinity of the prostitute led to this young man's downfall. Solomon's wise counsel to anyone entering this kind of tempting situation is, "My son, give me your heart, and let your eyes observe my ways. For a harlot is a deep pit" (Proverbs 23:26–27).

It's little wonder that the Bible tells us it is better to avoid tempting situations than to test our restraint. Here's the bottom line: "Do not enter the path of the wicked, and do not walk in the way of evil. Avoid it, do not travel on it; turn away from it and pass on" (Proverbs 4:14–15). Don't put one little toe on the path that leads to temptation; don't step on it, don't walk on it, don't go near it. Instead, turn from it and find God's way to spiritual success. John Dryden (1631–1700) gave this sage advice: "Better shun the bait than struggle in the snare." Avoiding a tempting situation isn't cowardice; it's common sense.

Avoid people who tempt you.

If you want to manage your temptation and learn how to be a spiritual success, avoiding tempting situations is only half the battle. Staying away from tempting people is the other half. Tempting people are those you take one look at and know immediately they are not going to advance your spiritual success.

As a college president for ten years, I constantly encouraged students to seek out friends who would help them up spiritually rather than drag them down. Our natural tendency is to apply a kind of spiritual second law of thermodynamics. That's the law that says everything is in atrophy; everything is winding down. We do much the same when we choose friends who have just a touch of larceny, friends who hint at an attractive dark side. They don't bring out the best in us; they draw us to temptation like a magnet. They drag us down spiritually. And yet we are somehow drawn to them.

You've experienced that, and so have I. The Bible contains many examples of people who chose the wrong kind of company and were lured into sin. "Do not be envious of evil men, nor desire to be with them; for their heart devises violence, and their lips talk of troublemaking" (Proverbs 24:1–2). Solomon's words were certainly prophetic. Rehoboam, who succeeded Solomon as king, lost his grandfather's kingdom by following the advice of the wrong friends (2 Chronicles 10). His young advisors dragged Rehoboam down spiritually.

It's not always easy to spot tempting people. That's why we need something of a *Life Guide to People Who Will Lead Us into Temptation*. Fortunately, we have such a guide. The Bible gives us insight into the wisdom of God, the will of God, and the way of God. The more we are in His Word and our lives are changed by it, the easier it is for us to spot a spiritual phony.

Solomon says to his sons that the wisdom found in God's Word will "deliver you from the way of evil, from the man who speaks perverse things, from those who leave the paths of uprightness to walk in the ways of darkness; who rejoice in doing evil, and delight in the perversity of the wicked; whose ways are crooked, and who are devious in their paths" (Proverbs 2:12–15).

How graphic a description of tempting people. Their words are wayward, ("Come on, we won't get caught"). They leave the straight and narrow paths (Matthew 7:13–14) to walk in crooked darkness (John 3:19). Tempting people do not tempt you because they are interested in you; they tempt you because they are interested in watching you fail ("What's the matter? Are you afraid?"). As Proverbs 11:20 says, "Those who are of a perverse heart are an abomination to the LORD, but the blameless in their ways are His delight." The Bible describes tempting people as perverse, crooked, devious. Is this the kind of person who will help you discover the secrets to spiritual success?

Avoid tempting liaisons.

Clearly the most frequent seduction that destroys our ability to manage temptation is sexual seduction. The list of godly people who have succumbed to tempting sexual liaisons reads like a Who's Who of failure. I don't need to remind you of their names; you can never forget them. And there are many more you have never heard of. They failed to avoid tempting situations and tempting people, and, as a result, that combination rocketed them headlong into sexual sin.

Among the sexual failures in the Bible are these giants—David (2 Samuel 11:4), Solomon (1 Kings 11:1), and Samson (Judges 16:1). There are also those with lesser reputations, but no lesser sins—Lot's daughters (Genesis 19:31), David's son Amnon (2 Samuel 13:11), and his son Absalom (2 Samuel 16:22). And there are many nameless sexual failures—the Israelites at Sinai (Exodus 32:28) and the church members at Corinth (1 Corinthians 5:1). Each failed to avoid tempting situations and tempting people and thus failed to avoid tempting liaisons.

The Samson scenario

Samson is the premier example of a giant who didn't control his temptations. In Judges 14:1, we read that Samson lusted after a Philistine woman, someone forbidden by God for any Israelite to marry, let alone an Israelite champion (Deuteronomy 7:3). That was his first recorded sexual liaison. It wouldn't be his last. In Judges 16:1, he went down to Gaza where he engaged a prostitute. And later in that chapter, he fell in love with the greatest temptress of all—Delilah. Three women in two chapters. Samson may have been an athletic bodybuilder, but he was a spiritual wimp. He was a physical champion, but a spiritual failure.

What was Samson's problem? He failed to appreciate the dangers of hanging around tempting places and tempting people. He didn't understand the wisdom of avoiding temptation rather than flirting with it. Maybe that's your problem, too.

Are you sliding down the path of Samson? Are you doing things, saying things, thinking things about a tempting person that you know could lead to a liaison? Have you touched a woman at the office in an inappropriate way? Have you said something suggestive to a man in your carpool? Have you enjoyed too close a relationship with someone who is not your spouse? Can you resist that temptation? David couldn't. Solomon couldn't. Samson couldn't. What makes you think you can? Millions of people who thought they could stop anytime found out they couldn't stop until it was too late.

Common sense

One of my favorite cartoon characters is the Roadrunner. Don't laugh. You can learn a lot about life from the Roadrunner and Wile E. Coyote. For example, when the coyote tries to trap his nemesis, he often piles bird seed along the side of the road. He even places a little sign with an arrow pointing to it that says "Bird Seed." When the Roadrunner comes by, he stops briefly at the bird seed, looks at it and, "Beep Beep," is on his way. He never gets caught. Never! And why? Because he is smart enough not to hang around what is obviously a trap set for him.

How different it is for Christians. Satan will place a little pile of tempting sin along the road, he even labels it "Sin," and, predictably, we hang around and hang around until eventually we are caught. Who is smarter? The Roadrunner who doesn't get caught or a Christian who does? I wish my buddy Dave had been more like the Roadrunner.

Here's the advice of God's Word: "Can a man take fire to his bosom, and his clothes not be burned? Can one walk on hot coals, and his feet not be seared? So is he who goes in to his neighbor's wife; whoever touches her shall not be innocent" (Proverbs 6:27–29). Temptation is a powerful tool in the arsenal of Satan. He is no fool who does all he can to avoid it.

When Temptation Threatens, Admit It

He was larger than life; so was she. He was charming, dashing, powerful. She was beautiful, innocent, lovable. He would be king of England, and she would be his queen. It was a fairy-tale romance. His name was Arthur; her name was Guinevere.

For everyone familiar with the story of Camelot, the love of Arthur for Guinevere and her love for him was story book material. Yet their happiness was ruined, their marriage destroyed, and their kingdom rocked by scandal. It started with an innocent look. Lancelot's eyes met Guinevere's. There was no premeditation to evil. It was all simple enough. But it was just a short, slippery step from a look to lust, from infatuation to infidelity. Their lives were ruined because they failed to manage their temptation.

When you live is no barrier to temptation.

He was larger than life; so was she. He was charming, dashing, powerful. She was beautiful, innocent, lovable. He would be king of England, and she would be his queen. It was a fairy-tale romance. His name was Charles; her name was Diana.

For everyone familiar with the story of Windsor, the similarities were all too striking. Perhaps you watched the wedding of the century on July 29, 1981. They seemed so much in love. Prince William was born less than a year later. Minor family squabbles appeared in the London tabloids over the next few years, but the House of Windsor had a devastating family secret. Both Charles and Di were reported to have had trysts throughout their marriage. In 1989, Charles vacationed in Turkey with Camilla Parker Bowles, without Princess Di. In a 1994 BBC TV interview, the man who would be king of England admitted his adultery. As for Diana, she carried on a five-year affair with James Hewitt, her riding instructor. Reportedly that wasn't the only one.

What destroyed these marriages? The failure to manage temptation. Time is not a factor in temptation. Whether the story is contemporary, rooted in English legend, or the Garden of Eden, temptation is a destroyer. No age since Eden has been exempt from Satan's tempting powers.

Temptation confronts kings and commoners.

Earlier I mentioned the range of biblical characters who were ensnared in sexual sin. Although King David's illicit affair is perhaps the most notorious case of succumbing to temptation, the problem certainly does not affect only the kingly class. The Bible features both kings and commoners—and everyone in between—who gave in to temptation. Lot gave in to the temptation to take what was best for himself rather than honor his uncle Abraham (Genesis 13). The result was a loss of his wife, his home, his possessions, and his honor. Achan was tempted to take things that were strictly forbidden to him (Joshua 7). He yielded, and the result was disgrace and death for him and his family. Cain was tempted by anger. When he gave in to this temptation, his brother lay dead on the ground and Cain became a marked man, hated wherever he went for the rest of his life (Genesis 4). These three represent a herdsman and wealthy man, a soldier and poor man, and a farmer and lonely man.

Nor is the problem of temptation limited to men. Miriam was tempted with power and position. When she yielded, her sin resulted in serious leprosy (Numbers 12). Martha gave in to the temptation of self-pity and worry, and that resulted in a gentle rebuke from the Lord Jesus (Luke 10). Naomi was tempted with bitterness and remained a widow the rest of her life (Ruth 1).

Falling to temptation is even a problem for couples. Ananias and Sapphira were tempted to mislead the Jerusalem church about their generosity, and that resulted in death for them both (Acts 5). The first patriarchal family, Abram and Sarai, were tempted to lie about being married, which brought about serious diseases on Pharaoh and his household (Genesis 12).

Men and women, couples and singles, ancient and modern, rich and poor, kingly and common, all were susceptible to temptation. Who you are is no guarantee that you won't be tempted, and it is certainly no guarantee that you won't fall to temptation.

The probability of success is no barrier to temptation.

Maybe you are saying to yourself, *I'm a mature Christian. Satan won't tempt me. He doesn't stand a chance. The likelihood of his success is minimal.* Don't think that will con Satan into letting you alone. He is the tempter; that's what he does. If he thought he could get Jesus to yield to temptation, what makes you think he won't come after you?

In fact, Matthew, chapter 4 tells that not only did Satan tempt Jesus, but he tried three times without success. In the desert temptation, he appealed to Jesus' hunger (the lust of the flesh). No deal. In the pinnacle temptation, he attempted to get Jesus to presume upon God (the pride of life). No deal again. And in the mountain temptation, he asked Jesus to look at all he could possess if he but fell down and worshiped Satan (the lust of the eyes). Still no deal.

No factor with Satan

Of all the lessons we can learn from these temptations (to quote Scripture when tempted, to resist Satan every time, to trust God for strength), perhaps the greatest is that the probability of success is never a factor in Satan's strategy. After the first failure with Jesus, you'd think Satan would expect to fail again. But he disregarded the probability of success and did his best to cajole Jesus into sin anyway. Some angels are slow learners.

Don't feel guilty when you are tempted. Temptation is a fact of life. It happens to everybody. In fact, if you aren't being tempted, it may be because the devil believes he already has you in his pocket. Your pastor is tempted; your parents are tempted; your spouse is tempted; no one is exempt. But being tempted is not sin. Yielding to temptation, that's the sin.

You are not a greater sinner for being tempted frequently. It only means you are only more frequently targeted by the devil. You are only a greater sinner if you give in to temptation frequently. That's an important distinction that you must make, or your chances of spiritual success will diminish dramatically.

TO RESTRAIN TEMPTATION, UNDERSTAND IT

The Six-Day War in June of 1967 lasted, well, six days. Israeli tanks and artillery, accompanied by the mighty Israeli air force, completely overran Israel's neighbors in a blitzkrieg war unparalleled in history. But the secret to Israel's success was much more than military superiority. The Persian Gulf War in 1991 likewise was brief. U.S. and Allied forces humiliated Saddam Hussein by outfoxing him, outgunning him, and outfighting him. And again, the secret to the success of the coalition forces was much more than military superiority.

Ask any general or war strategist what the greatest weapon in warfare is, and he will tell you that it's military intelligence. Knowing beforehand how your enemy thinks, what strategies he intends to employ, where and when he is apt to strike, not only allows you to mount a successful defense but also enables you to go on offense against him. If this is true in physical warfare, why would it not be equally true in spiritual warfare?

Simply admitting that you're going to be tempted is not enough. You must understand the stratagems and methods of your enemy, the devil. Paul warned the Corinthian church that if they wanted to prevent Satan from outwitting them, they must be aware of the devil's devices (2 Corinthians 2:11). You may not understand everything about Satan and his schemes, but the Bible gives you a lot of insight about him and how he operates. Use that insight to manage the temptation in your life. Here are some of the major lessons spiritually successful people have learned about the devil and his devices.

"Subtle" is Satan's pseudonym.

From day one, Satan chose to demonstrate his cunning superiority over mankind. He used his subtlety as a weapon against Adam and Eve in Eden's Garden. Satan chose not to approach Eve in his usual devil duds. Instead, as a serpent, he slithered up on Eve. The story of the fall is recorded in Genesis 3, which begins, "Now the serpent was more cunning than any beast of the field which the LORD God had made" (v. 1). A subtle Satan masqueraded as a subtle snake. If you're going to manage the temptation in your life, don't expect the devil to play fair. He won't.

Norman "Kid" McCoy was the welterweight boxing champion in 1896. In one of his fights, the contender was deaf. McCoy discovered his opponent's disability and wasted no time in using it to his advantage. Near the end of the third round, McCoy stepped back a pace, dropped his arms and pointed to his opponent's corner, indicating that the bell had rung. Of course the bell hadn't rung, and as soon as his adversary dropped his arms and turned away, McCoy cold-cocked him, leaving him in a heap on the canvas.

It sounds like the "Kid" had Satan for a mentor. He tempts us in the same way. He approaches us as subtly as he can, exploiting every advantage he has over us. Eternal vigilance is not only the price of liberty; in our warfare with principalities and powers, it is the price of spiritual success. Never let your guard down, even when Satan convinces you that you are in no danger. Satan is not a model of sportsmanship.

Satan is content to operate slowly.

This may surprise you, but the devil is in no hurry to tempt you. He would rather be successful than speedy. So he'll take his time to lay a trap for you. He'll slink into the bushes and watch you for hours or even days before he makes his move. He'll watch the clock and say to himself, *Slow down, Lucifer. Everything comes to those who wait.* You don't ever have to worry about the devil risking success by springing the trap too soon. He is very patient in temptation.

Often coworkers of my friend Dave heard him make snide remarks about the women in his office. For years he was guilty of making innuendoes and comments that could be taken two ways. He would mix an off-color comment with a complement. And he had been doing it for years. Nobody liked it, but everybody expected it. Dave and Cindy's affair didn't begin instantaneously. Their affection didn't develop in a hurry. It took months before the glances and the comments became the ill-advised meetings in the lunchroom. Satan was in no hurry to ensnare Dave and Cindy. He knew he could take his time. In fact, so slowly did this relationship develop that they saw it as no big deal, until it exploded and ruined both their lives.

Satan often softens us up before he strikes. He's no dummy. He knows we'll be more susceptible to his attacks if we are not in tip-top spiritual shape. So he pummels us slowly; he softens us slowly; he prepares us slowly for the kill. He's like the little boy being interviewed on TV. When asked if he had any pets, the boy replied, "Well, I did have some goldfish, but some water softener got into the aquarium, and they got softened to death." Often the devil simply softens us to death.

Watch out when Satan is making life too easy for you. Self-indulgence, laziness, indifference toward God and His Word, a lack of self-discipline—these are all ways Satan slowly prepares us for his knockout punch. It may take some time, but make no mistake about it. If you don't manage temptation in your life, a knockout is coming.

Satan is the master of proportion.

The old devil has been in the temptation business long enough to know that we aren't going to jump off the end of the pier into sin. That's why Satan comes to us slowly when he tempts us. He also comes proportionately. He spoon-feeds us in such a way that we don't get too much at one time. Satan knows that if we gulp too big a dose of sin, we may find it repulsive and spit it out. So that sneaky snake gives us a little here and a little there until we're hooked.

Have you ever watched a cow wander away from the herd? It's not that the cow sees a nice patch of meadow on the other side of the stream and makes a beeline for it. No, the cow starts nibbling on a tuft of green grass; it looks ahead to another tuft, and then another and another. Little by little, it has nibbled itself lost. Christians are a lot like cows in this way. When it comes to sin, we don't take too big of a bite. There are usually no big gulps of grass. We just nibble ourselves lost.

Certainly this is what Satan did with Eve in the Garden. He presented himself to her as a snake. She nibbled. Planting doubt in her mind, he asked, "Has God indeed said, 'You shall not eat of every tree of the garden'?" (Genesis 3:1). Munch. Munch. Eve answered the serpent's question without a hint of rebuke about its derogatory inference concerning God's goodness (v. 2). Nibble. Nibble. Finally, Satan called God a liar: "You will not surely die" (v. 4). Eve listened to Satan's lie. Chomp. Chomp. Eve was being tempted by Satan and didn't even know it. He was moving subtly, slowly, and proportionately until she nibbled herself lost.

If you detect Satan doing this with you, don't follow Eve's example. Cut Satan off. Stop him in his tracks. Don't listen anymore. Tell him to slither away. We rarely jump into sin on the first encounter. We just nibble and nibble until we nibble ourselves lost. As John Ray observed in the seventeenth century: "Feather by feather the goose is plucked."

Watch out for pretty packaging.

Think of all those pretty packages under your tree at Christmas. There's the one your wife bought for you. But it is wrapped in an old brown grocery bag (the only wrapping my father ever used at Christmas). Not very appealing, but inside is your treasure, something you've wanted for a long time. Another present from your wife is attractively wrapped, tied with a bow and curly ribbons. It just cries out, "Open me. Open me." But inside is your wife's "Honey do" jar (Honey, do this; Honey, do that). The packaging is very appealing, but inside are a hundred ways to spoil your Saturday. So, which will you open? It depends on your ability to manage temptation.

Satan is a master salesman. If he were in real estate, he'd be a million-dollar agent year after year. If he were a used car salesman, he'd be salesman of the month. The devil knows how to package temptation so that it just screams at you, "Open me. Open me."

Think of all the ways Satan packages temptation to get you hooked. Often he makes the package small because he knows small things intrigue us. Don't big things come in small packages? Francis of Sales, a sixteenth-century saint, observed: "For every great temptation there will be many small ones. Wolves and bears are more dangerous than flies, but we are bothered most by flies." Satan is the master of the small package.

Satan wraps his tempting packages with just a hint of mystique and vice to make them alluring. In Christian circles, secretaries often aren't tempted with their boss's power, nor are bosses often tempted with their secretary's beauty, so much as they are tempted with the scintillation of a little sinfulness. An office romance may develop between the pastor and his secretary simply because that relationship is beyond the bounds of propriety. They risk everything because of the thrill of a little lechery. Satan is the master at stirring feelings because they are taboo. The first-century Roman historian Tacitus hit the nail on the head when he said, "Things forbidden have a secret charm." Satan makes sure of it.

We must take care not to choose a present because of the wrapping. The devil is not bound by a "truth in advertising" law. Often Satan's packaging is the only thrill there is, but if we do not understand the subtlety of Satan's tactics, we are sure to yield to temptation and be greatly disappointed—not to mention severely judged by God. Understand your enemy's illusions, or spiritual success will elude you forever.

To Defeat Temptation, Let the Spirit Do It

Let's face it, you and I don't stand a chance. We are doomed. If we have to match wits with Satan, we will be outwitted. If we have to match our power with that powerful angel, we will be outwatted. Satan is a formidable enemy, a crafty devil. We are no match for him by ourselves.

Fortunately, we don't face him by ourselves. Our spiritual success doesn't depend on our power, our intelligence, or just plain good luck. It depends on our ability to tap resources that are not our own. Managing temptation depends to a great extent on our letting the Spirit of God do it for us.

Resource available

The resource of the Holy Spirit—His power and strength—is available to everyone who has trusted Jesus Christ as Savior. That's what the Bible says. At the very moment of our salvation, the Holy Spirit takes up residence within us. He actually lives in our body; it becomes the living quarters of the Holy Spirit (1 Corinthians 6:19). That means we take Him with us wherever we go, even into the jaws of temptation.

Here are some of the Bible's promises with regard to the Holy Spirit being a resource available to you twenty-four hours a day:

- The Holy Spirit is God's promised gift to all who believe (John 14:26–27).
- He takes up His residence in us upon salvation and indwells His people (John 14:16).
- Thus, it would be impossible to be saved and not have the Holy Spirit (Romans 8:9).
- Since the Spirit lives in us, not only does He enable us to serve the Lord acceptably (Acts 1:8), but He empowers us to wage war against our spiritual enemies (Galatians 5:16).

If you want to manage temptation successfully, don't forget the Superhero living inside you. Give the control of tantalizing thoughts, troubling situations, and tempting people over to the Spirit within you, and let Him work in your behalf.

How to activate your resources

Here's how to put the Spirit of God to work for you in resisting the devil and managing temptation:

1. *Ask the Holy Spirit to make you aware of Satan's main arenas for temptation.* You do this by reading God's Word and letting the Spirit teach you practical lessons from it (John 14:26). Read and compare the great temptation passage of the Old Testament (Genesis 3:1–6) with the great temptation passage of the New Testament (Matthew 4:1–11). When you do, you'll notice that Satan's temptations always come in three arenas: "the lust of the flesh, the lust of the eyes, and the pride of life" (1 John 2:16).

Satan often appeals to legitimate desires. What he wanted Jesus to do was not wrong per se. It was natural for Jesus to be hungry after a forty-day fast, to want to descend safely from the pinnacle of the temple, and to validate His legitimate claim to all the kingdoms of the world. What was wrong was the timing and the way Satan wanted Him to respond to legitimate desires.

That will be true for you as well. Much of what tempts you will be normal, things in the everyday course of life. The Spirit of God will help you discern what is temptation from Satan and what is legitimate from God. If you allow the Spirit of God to inform you about where Satan is active in your life, you have taken a giant step in managing that temptation.

2. *Let the Holy Spirit teach you from God's Word on a consistent basis so you have the right ammunition to shoot down temptation.* Are you as impressed as I am that each time Jesus was tempted, He responded by quoting Scripture? Imagine how much more difficult managing temptation would have been if Jesus had no command of God's Word. Imagine how much more difficult it would be for you if you haven't tucked away some Scripture in your heart and mind.

The antidote to giving in to temptation is allowing the Spirit of God to impress the Word of God on the people of God at just the right moment. "Your word is a lamp to my feet and a light to my path" (Psalm 119:105). "Your word I have hidden in my heart, that I might not sin against You" (Psalm 119:11). But since you can't know the moment when temptation will strike, you have to be prepared all the time. The Holy Spirit can help. Get into a reading program that will take you through the Bible in a year. Ask the Holy Spirit to help you both to internalize the Word and memorize it for later use against Satan.

3. *Adjust to the presence of the Holy Spirit in your life and let Him have His way.* Look at Jesus. There is a pervasive and powerful presence of the Spirit of the Living God in every aspect of Jesus' life. As Millard J. Erickson explains, "Jesus was led by the Holy Spirit into the situation where the temptation took place. Mark's statement is forceful: 'The Spirit immediately drove him out into the wilderness' (1:12). Jesus is virtually 'expelled' by the Spirit."[7] Luke tells us that following the temptation, "Jesus returned in the power of the Spirit to Galilee" (4:14).

Two things are obvious. First, if Jesus' life was under the influence and control of the Holy Spirit and He is God, shouldn't our lives be under the control of the Spirit if we want to be successful? And second, being under the control of the Spirit meant Jesus often was led into places of temptation. That will be true for you, too. Don't worry. "He who is in you is greater than he who is in the world" (1 John 4:4). Just do what Jesus did—let the Spirit impress His divine will upon you and have the courage to follow it.

4. *Join the Spirit in praying that you will not enter the path of temptation.* If you keep off the path, you stay away from the problem. The Lord's Prayer includes that plaintive request, "And do not lead us into temptation, but deliver us from the evil one" (Matthew 6:13). Ask the Lord to guide your steps so that you do not wander into the paths that lead to Satan and sin.

Jesus said it another way in Matthew 26:41: "Watch and pray, lest you enter into temptation." Be vigilant about where your feet take you, what your eyes look at, what your mind thinks about, and pray that in none of these things you will lose your ability to manage temptation. Vigilance and prayer. The Holy Spirit will help with both. Let Him keep you alert through the Word and ask Him to pray for your release from tempting situations and people. After all, prayer is one of the Spirit's major ministries (Romans 8:26–27).

5. *Rely on the Spirit's faithfulness to help you resist temptation.* Use God's escape hatch from temptation. "No temptation has overtaken you except such as is common to man; but God is faithful, who will not allow you to be tempted beyond what you are able, but with the temptation will also make the way of escape, that you may be able to bear it" (1 Corinthians 10:13). The "way of escape" promised here is the internal help of the Holy Spirit. He gives us strength that is not our own (1 John 4:4).

God has made a way, but too many of us fail to take it. God left an avenue of escape for my friend Dave. One day at work a colleague of Dave's asked him to step into his office. Fred did not attend the same church as Dave, but he knew that Dave at least professed to be a Christian. Fred was blunt.

"What's going on?" Fred asked.

Dave played dumb, "What do you mean?"

"You know full well what I mean. What's going on between Cindy and you? Everybody in the office sees what's happening, man."

That confrontation could have been the escape hatch for Dave, but he didn't take it. Instead of pulling the handle on the ejection seat, Dave crashed and burned with Cindy. Dave failed to ask the Spirit of God to help him during those months of temptation because, frankly, Dave didn't want help. He was enjoying the temptation so much that he was blinded to the consequences. Now it's too late.

The internal presence of the Spirit of God in your life will help you understand and put into practice the promise of James 4:7: "Therefore submit to God. Resist the devil and he will flee from you." When you adjust your life to the presence of the Spirit of God, you are submitting yourself to God. When you ask Him to help you resist the devil, you'll successfully resist the devil. But when you try to do it by yourself, you fail to manage temptation and Satan manages you. It's a no-brainer. The Spirit is faithful to help you win out over temptation if you rely on Him. But you are powerless to manage temptation if you don't seek His help in watching and praying.

Temptation is not just for the weak; it arrives at the doorstep of the pastor, the priest, and the rabbi. It attacks the scholar and the socialite. It is a problem for the stay-at-home mom and the career woman. Temptation is a universal problem. It knows no racial, national, or denominational boundaries.

If you can get a handle on the temptations that plague you, you can grip the handle of success in your Christian life. But even if temptation comes crashing in on us, all is not lost.

Success Survey #5

1. *How do you respond to temptation?* Being tempted is no sign of weakness; yielding to temptation is the sign of spiritual weakness. So, when you are tempted, how often do you yield? Be brutally honest with yourself. When the opportunity comes to do something that you know displeases God, do you often take it? How much of the time? Do you rationalize and say, "Everybody does it"? Do you spiritualize and say, "This isn't Satan; this is God giving me the go ahead"? Or do you deal with temptation in a way that proves you are growing strong spiritually?

2. *What is your greatest point of weakness?* You can prepare for temptation by knowing where you are most likely to fall. Satan knows, so why shouldn't you? What are the areas of life you know you have the most difficulty with? Name them. Get a clear picture in your head of where your spiritual defenses are weakest. Do you have a defense prepared against those areas where you are most likely to slip?

3. *Who are the people you must avoid?* How easy is it for you to avoid people and places that tempt you? Probably not very easy. But is it possible? Probably. So what will you do today to avoid temptation? Who is that person at work who seems to be a bit too friendly? What is your plan to avoid the individual? God has given you both common sense and a spiritual way to escape every temptation. Which will you fail to use and thus fail to manage temptation? Identify clearly who and what you should be avoiding.

4. *How do you know when you're being tempted?* Is it possible you're being tempted and you aren't even aware of it? Or do you think you are somehow exempt from temptation? That could be dangerous. If Jesus was not exempt from temptation, why would you be? How skillful are you at discerning temptation? How do you determine if you are being tempted? What does it make you feel like when you are tempted? What do others say? Strange as it may seem, temptation can be so subtle it disguises itself as friendship until it's too late. The trap is sprung and we are caught. Can you really identify temptation?

5. *What is your "yield ratio"?* What percentage of the times you know you are tempted do you respond by walking away? What percentage of the times do you fall? Do you give in 10 percent of the time? 50 percent? even more? If you think your yield ratio is far too high, perhaps you should reread this chapter before you move on to the next one. The place to stop temptation is when you first realize you are being tempted. If you haven't been doing that, the chances are your yield ratio is worse than you think.

SPIRITUAL SECRET #6

If You Fall, Don't Stay Down

There are no victories at bargain prices.
DWIGHT D. EISENHOWER

If you faint in the day of adversity, your strength is small.
PROVERBS 24:10

—◦◦◦—

The Christian life is a battle. No surprise there. We are engaged in mortal combat with an enemy we can't even see. As Ephesians 6:12 tells us, "For our struggle is not against flesh and blood, but against the rulers, against the authorities, against the powers of this dark world and against the spiritual forces of evil in the heavenly realms" (NIV). And while it is possible to manage temptation and defeat Satan in our struggle for spiritual success, let's face it—we don't always win. Occasionally, we are overrun by the enemy.

You've taken all the precautions. You've read the manual, and you know Satan's strategy. You knew that pretty wrapping meant it was the devil's "present," but you couldn't help yourself. Like a kid at Christmas, you had to sneak a peek. You knew you shouldn't, but you did. You were well aware of the consequences, but your lust overwhelmed you. Like my buddy Dave whom I told about in the last chapter, you knew this would ruin your life, but you just didn't care. You slipped into sin and found yourself face down on the mat. It wasn't supposed to be this way, but it is. So, now what?

Let me encourage you. Remember one thing when you fall: You've got to get up because the war isn't over. When it is, you will be in the victory parade. When the fighting is over, when all the battles are fought, we know who wins the war. We do! Praise God. We've read the last chapter of the Book and the Bridegroom (Jesus Christ) gets the Bride (His Church), and they live happily ever after. We know we will ultimately win the war.

I draw unbelievable courage and hope from Paul's words in Romans

8:35–39: "Who shall separate us from the love of Christ? Shall tribulation, or distress, or persecution, or famine, or nakedness, or peril, or sword?...Yet in all these things we are more than conquerors through Him who loved us. For I am persuaded that neither death nor life, nor angels nor principalities nor powers, nor things present nor things to come, nor height nor depth, nor any other created thing, shall be able to separate us from the love of God which is in Christ Jesus our Lord."

Don't miss the powerful message in these verses. It doesn't matter how much Satan tries to halt the progress of your spiritual journey, it doesn't matter how often he succeeds and you stumble and fall, God loves you and will ultimately make you more than conquerors through Christ Jesus. That's a promise to hang onto when you aren't as successful in managing temptation as you would like to be.

SPIRITUAL PARALYSIS

What do Christopher Reeve, Joni Eareckson Tada, and Paul Goode all have in common? Well, if you knew Paul, you'd quickly say that all three are victims of paralysis. Christopher Reeve was Superman, literally. In the *Superman* movies, he played the man of steel. He was an athletic, strikingly handsome actor. Then one day a few years ago a riding accident left him paralyzed from the neck down. Now when you see him, you see a strikingly handsome man in a wheelchair, with rigid posture.

Joni Eareckson Tada's story is much the same. A vibrant young girl, Joni was injured in a diving accident and became quadriplegic. Today you may know her through her writings, music, artwork, public appearances, or her JAF Ministries radio program. Ever vibrant and joyful, Joni will never walk again.

And Paul Goode? You've never heard of him. But I see him all the time in his wheelchair, struggling to hold his head erect at the corner of a busy intersection in Lincoln, Nebraska. He's usually pushing the button on the traffic light to stop the traffic and give him enough time to wheel his way across the street. Paul, too, is a victim of paralysis.

When we see those who are physically paralyzed, it always incites both sympathy and gratitude—sympathy for their struggles to live a normal life and gratitude that we have full use of our bodies. But often when someone becomes spiritually paralyzed, our response is less sympathetic and more condemning. How unlike Jesus with the woman who was guilty of adultery. He did not condone her sin, but He demonstrated significant compassion for her as a sinner: "Neither do I condemn you; go and sin no more" (John 8:11).

A COMMON MALADY

Spiritual paralysis is a common problem. Frequently, it happens like this: You have been living your Christian life the best you know how. You've been getting advice from your pastor and friends at the Bible study group. You've been reading your Bible and growing consistently. And, yes, you've been sensing that temptation and difficulty in your life are on the rise. Expect it. Satan doesn't like to lose. And along the way, some temptation broadsides you when you aren't looking. You are hit in a weak moment and you give in. You stumble and fall into sin. It's happened to all of us.

But here's where things really begin to deteriorate. You're knocked down in your sin, you struggle, but you can't get up. You try again, but somehow Satan knows all the choke holds, and he keeps you down. You're pretty sure you're down for the count, so after a while you stop struggling and just give up. The result? Spiritual paralysis.

Spiritual paralysis is not falling into sin or giving in to temptation—it is not getting back up when you've been knocked down.

The Bible is filled with examples of people afflicted by spiritual paralysis. Lot, nephew of Abraham, the friend of God, had imbibed much of the spiritual strength of his uncle. But when he moved into the city of Sodom and became insensitive to the sin around him, he became spiritually paralyzed. You can read his story in Genesis 19. So paralyzed was Lot that when two angels in the form of men were sent from God to deliver him from the Sodom cesspool, Lot made some decidedly unspiritual decisions. When the homosexuals of Sodom came banging on his door angrily demanding that the two men be brought out so they could abuse them sexually, Lot offered to give them his own daughters, hoping to satisfy the sexual desires of these depraved Sodomites (v. 8). This man was so spiritually paralyzed that he couldn't think straight. He was down, and he couldn't get up.

The same thing happened to the prophet Jonah. After God rescued Jonah from the belly of the fish, God gave him a second chance. Again God called this wayward prophet to go to Nineveh and preach a message of repentance to the Ninevites. This time Jonah obeyed, but when God saved the entire city because they repented of their sin, Jonah complained that he knew God was gracious and merciful, slow to anger and abundant in lovingkindness (Jonah 4:2). The prophet just knew God would forgive the people Jonah hated so much; therefore, when his bitterness knocked him down, he couldn't get back up. He was spiritually paralyzed. The book of Jonah ends with Jonah angry at God.

What about Diotrephes in the New Testament? He's the guy who was upset with the apostle John because he thought John had too much influence over the church. Diotrephes wanted to be the Big Kahuna and when that didn't happen, he slipped some vicious stories to the church about John and tried to undermine his authority. That's how he stumbled and fell into sin, but he never got up again. The tiny epistle of 3 John records Diotrephes' antics and John's counsel to the members of the church: "Do not imitate what is evil, but what is good" (v. 11).

STILL A PROBLEM TODAY

Of course, falling and not getting up was not a problem in Bible times only. There are plenty of Christians today who have not managed temptation well, have fallen into sin, and have failed to get up again. All we have to do is look around us.

I have a distant relative who has a brother living in a neighboring state. My relative's brother—I'll call him John—is probably twenty years my senior, but we have always been close. He's a terrifically nice guy. John was a handsome, happy-go-lucky bachelor. He had plenty of dates when he was younger, but he never found the right girl. John had impeccable taste and unachievable standards for the woman he would marry. Consequently, he never met anyone who could meet those standards.

John filled his life with his work, his boat, his love for adventure. He always had a flashy convertible, a wallet full of cash, and what appeared to be an enviable life. But John is a lonely man. Beneath that happy exterior is a whole lot of empty. John is a Christian, but his life has been filled with unbelievable pain and sorrow. John used to attend church regularly, but after a series of minor spiritual failures, he stopped going. He also stopped reading his Bible. In fact, John's spiritual journey has come to a virtual standstill. Some years ago, John slipped into sin with one of his dates and opted to pay for an abortion. He has deeply felt the guilt of that decision. John has had several nervous breakdowns and is chemically being treated for depression. His spiritual life is a mess.

John has sought help from counselors and others. I have spent hours with him trying to help him up off the mat, where he lies limp in spiritual defeat. John suffers from what many Christians suffer from, something we might call "spiritual vertigo." He tries to get up from his spiritual defeats, but he is light-headed and dizzy. He can't quite get it together. He is woozy and faint like a boxer who has taken one too many blows to the skull. When he makes his move to get up off the mat and take on Satan again, John collapses in an unsteady heap.

Maybe your spiritual journey is not at a standstill like John's, but have you spent a lot of time on the mat? Have you been down so long that you can't remember when you were up? Are you tired of your lack of progress as a Christian? Have some menacing sins been keeping you defeated? It doesn't have to be that way. You can bounce back if you just get up when you fall.

HOW TO HANDLE SPIRITUAL FAILURE

If you have taken all the steps to manage temptation but still have become embroiled in it, what can you do? How can you rebound from a fall? There is a way. It's God's way. Here's what the Bible says you can do to get up and get back on the road to spiritual success.

Admit your sin.

Admitting sin is not easy; it shouldn't be. If it were easy, we'd do it capriciously. We admit sin because we can do no less. It's the first step back from the abyss. It's the only way to clear our conscience and become right with God. Without a clear, heartfelt admission of sin, guilt festers and ultimately destroys us. So if you don't want to stay down, admit your sin and let God help you up.

The Bible records life as it really is. It doesn't hide a thing. When men and women sinned against the holy God, the writers of the Bible wrote about it. David's adultery with Bathsheba was not swept under the rug. Lot's incest with his daughters was not hidden. Peter's repeated faux pas of faith were recorded for us to learn from them. But just as the Bible recorded the sins of men and women, so, too, it recorded their admissions of guilt. Often you read of Bible characters saying those three little words that are so difficult: "I have sinned."

- Aaron said them (Numbers 12:11).
- Balaam said them (Numbers 22:34).
- Achan said them (Joshua 7:20).
- Shimei said them (2 Samuel 19:20).
- King Saul said them several times (1 Samuel 15:24, 30; 26:21).
- So did King David (2 Samuel 12:13; 24:10, 17; Psalm 41:4).

I suppose the people of God, collectively, hold the *Guinness* record for the number of times they had to cough up an admission of sin. Just a few of the times they said "We have sinned" are recorded in Numbers 14:40; Deuteronomy 1:41; Judges 10:10; 1 Samuel 7:6; Nehemiah 1:6; Psalm 106:6; Isaiah 42:24; Jeremiah 3:25; Lamentations 5:7; Daniel 9:8, and the list goes on.

Admitting you have sinned is the initial step in getting back on your spiritual journey after you've been down on the mat. Just make sure you mean it when you say the words. Some of King Saul's admissions of guilt may be questionable, and all of the times Pharaoh said "I have sinned" were insincere (Exodus 9:27; 10:16). You can't fool God with an insincere admission of guilt. The pain of admission is severe, but not nearly as severe as the pain and consequences of failing to admit sin.

Show remorse for your sin.

Trying to glibly admit sin without showing any remorse is a human response. Presidents do it; so do kings. David initially did that, but when confronted, he showed genuine remorse and said, "For I acknowledge my transgressions, and my sin is always before me. Against You, You only, have I sinned, and done this evil in Your sight—that You may be found just when You speak, and blameless when You judge" (Psalm 51:3–4). Remorse is the telltale sign of a true admission of guilt. How will people know when you are genuine in admitting your sin? What are the signs of remorse?

When Nehemiah heard that the wall of his beloved Jerusalem was still in disrepair years after the repatriation of the land, before he prayed to confess the sins of his nation, he sat down and wept and mourned for many days and fasted (Nehemiah 1:4). These are signs of remorse. During the Babylonian captivity, Daniel prayed his impassioned prayer of confession for his nation. But he preceded his prayer by fasting, donning sackcloth, and dowsing his head with ashes (Daniel 9:3)—all signs of remorse.

When we see how devastating, destructive, and damning sin is, our guilt should tear our heart. When we genuinely come to grips with the heinousness of sin, it will always drive us to shame. That's what happened to Adam and Eve...and David...and the prodigal son. If we fail to exhibit this kind of gut-wrenching shame, it may be because we have made no real admission of guilt.

Confess your sin.

What does it mean to confess sin? The Bible says, "If we confess our sins, He is faithful and just to forgive us our sins and to cleanse us from all unrighteousness" (1 John 1:9). What a reassuring promise. God's character is such that He will never fail to forgive us and wipe the slate clean of our unrighteous behavior if we do just one thing—confess. You can see, then, how important it is to know what confession means. Forgiveness and cleansing depend on it.

When John said, "If we confess our sins," he used the Greek word *homologeo*. This is the only place in the Bible where the word is used. It is a composite word made up of two root words: *homou*, meaning together or an assembly of people (John 21:2); and *logos*, meaning word or saying (Matthew 19:22). The combined meaning is evident: It means to say the same thing as another, to say together, to agree with.

When you confess your sins, you say the same thing as your accuser. Suppose you were guilty of dumping trash on a remote corner of your neighbor's property. If he confronted you about your dubious dumping, and you confessed, you would say the same thing your neighbor was saying. You would say, "Yep, I did it. I dumped my trash on your property." You would agree with his accusation, concede your sin, and assent to your guilt. You wouldn't rationalize; you'd own up to your actions.

You don't excuse your sin because everybody dumps there. You don't blame your neighbor for being an aggressive investigator. You're the one at fault, and you say what your neighbor is saying. It's true. You did it. That's confession.

Failure to admit sin, be remorseful for it, and confess it means that you have to hide your sin, you have to divert blame, you have to dilute the language of your offense. On the other hand, confessing sin opens wide the door for forgiveness and cleansing. The choice is yours.

Recognize against whom you have sinned.

Most people apparently don't understand the nature of sin. Two teenage girls shoplift from the local department store and rationalize, "It's not hurting anybody. It's a big company; they can afford it." A mugger mars the face of an innocent victim and says, "It's not my problem. She shouldn't have been standing there." Still others fail to declare all their earnings on their income tax forms and shrug off their behavior: "Everybody cheats on their income tax." It's all symptomatic, isn't it? Sin is usually thought of as nondirectional. It isn't specifically targeted. Even in cases of date rape, there is a tendency to downplay the relationship with the victim.

We will never feel shame for our sin until we recognize against whom we have sinned. When you sin against your parents, they are not the ultimate target of your sin. When you sin against your spouse or your friends, they, too, are not the final target of your sin. When you slander your pastor, bad-mouth your boss, or discriminate against your neighbor, they are not where your sin ends. God is!

Our failure to understand that we ultimately sin against God is one of the reasons we sin with such a cavalier attitude. We just don't realize against whom we are sinning. What does the Bible say? These examples will show us.

Joseph in Egypt

When Joseph, son of Jacob, was sold into slavery by his brothers, he was purchased by a wealthy Egyptian named Potiphar. When Potiphar's wife got a good look at this young, handsome Hebrew, she attempted to seduce him. In refusing to sin with his master's wife, the innocent Joseph demonstrated he knew a lot about the ultimate target of sin. He said, "How then can I do this great wickedness, and sin against God?" (Genesis 39:9). There was not a word about sinning against himself, or the wife, or even Potiphar. To have yielded to this woman would have been sin involving all three individuals, but Joseph didn't even mention them. His concern was that he would sin against God, because all sin is ultimately always directed against God.

David in Jerusalem

When King David gave in to his lust and slept with Bathsheba, he obviously sinned against her. She was a married woman; this was adultery. He also sinned against himself, the man after God's own heart. And obviously he sinned against Bathsheba's husband, Uriah the Hittite, because he died as a result of David's futile attempt to cover up his sin. But when David made his painful admission and confession of sin, this is what he said: "Have mercy upon me, O God.... Against You, You only have I sinned, and done this evil in Your sight" (Psalm 51:1, 4). What about Bathsheba? What about David? More to the point, what about Uriah? Didn't David sin against them as well? Of course he did, but the king understood that all sin is ultimately against God.

The prodigal son

Jesus' great parable of the prodigal teaches the same truth—God is the real object of our sin. When the prodigal was far from home, out of money and in trouble, he finally realized how foolish he had been and he returned home. He confessed to his father, "I have sinned against heaven and in your sight, and am no longer worthy to be called your son" (Luke 15:21). Besides the obvious remorse and repentance in the boy's confession, did you notice that he claimed to have sinned "against heaven" as well as "in your sight"? What did he mean? The prodigal realized that even though he had hurt his father, he had egregiously sinned against God.

Saul of Tarsus

Ranting and raving about how Christians had perverted the Jewish religion, Saul of Tarsus set out from Jerusalem to Damascus to haul back to the capital city anyone who had trusted Jesus as Messiah and Savior. Remember, Saul was after people—people he thought were destroying the purity of his religion. But when that bright light shone down and a voice from heaven spoke, it did not say, "Saul, Saul, why are you persecuting My people?" It said, "Why are you persecuting Me?" (Acts 9:3).

To be successful in your Christian life, you have to come to some conclusions about sin. One of those conclusions is that sin is serious because all sin is ultimately directed against God. While you may hurt others in the process of your sin, and you must make it right with them, you ultimately hurt God and your relationship with Him. That's what makes sin so damaging to us.

Retrace your steps.

When you have bottomed out in your sin, it's time to go back and retake your lost ground. How do you know when you've bottomed out? When you can't go any farther, when you can't sink any deeper, when you can't feel any more guilty, you've bottomed out. The prodigal son was like that when he was feeding the pigs and discovered that a Jewish boy couldn't get much lower. The boy bottomed out. It happened to David when he realized that there was no sense adding any other sin to adultery and murder. David bottomed out.

Conversely, you can always tell when a sinner hasn't yet bottomed out. They continue to misdirect the blame for their sin; they continue to misrepresent what they did; they continue to fail to demonstrate any remorse.

So once you've come to the end of your rope, what do you do? Tie a knot there so you don't slip any farther, take a minute to catch your breath, and then ask God to help you climb out of the hole you've dug for yourself. You have to retrace the steps that got you into this mess in the first place. Here's how.

Make a time line of events.

Start where you are and work backward. Create a reverse timeline of the events that took you to the end of your rope. Get a piece of paper and write down the steps that led you to where you are. Be sure to include people, places, and events. One of them may trigger your memory that will eventually lead you to forgiveness and cleansing. You need to get the facts down and make sure they are accurate.

Make a list of every place you've been where you've failed to manage temptation. Include your church, job, home, friends' homes, everywhere. Don't forget the out-of-the-way places like restaurants, ball games, the gym, or vacation spots. Write everything down. You can discard later what is immaterial to retracing your steps. You need to get a working timeline of people, places, and events so you are sure you've covered all the bases.

Make a "People to talk to" list.

When confessing sin, you always begin with God. But God is like the center concentric circle when you throw a stone into a pond. He's the center ring. But the rings emanate out and send shockwaves through the community. You need to speak with anyone you have involved in your failure.

When Douglas, an executive in a major firm, was accused by fellow workers of having an affair, Janet "just knew it was true." The only female executive in the company, Janet had been irritated with Douglas as the two had locked horns over policies and procedures for months. As her pastor would later describe it, what Janet did *seem* spiritual. She called fifteen of her closest friends at work and at church (where she, Douglas, and their spouses both attended). She shared her concerns about the rumors of the affair.

She told them, "Now, I'm not gossiping. I'm calling because I'm concerned. I think we need to pray for Douglas, and if this is true—and I suspect it is—we need to ask God to help him repent and put his life back together."

Janet may have thought she wasn't gossiping, but she was. If you were guilty of spreading a nasty rumor about your neighbor, as Janet was about Douglas, God is at the center of that hurt, but your neighbor is right behind Him. And what about the other neighbors who you maliciously informed when you spread that rumor? They were affected by it, too. What about the people at church with whom you subtly shared this rumor as a "prayer request"? You've got to speak to them, too. The list may get long. Better to have a long complete list, however, than a short, incomplete one. I wonder how long Janet's list should be?

Confession and concentric circles

Often I am asked about making public confessions of sin. Is it necessary? Is it even advisable? Sin is a dirty business and must be cleaned up. So when you make your confession of sin to others, do it this way.

If you have sinned privately against someone and your sin extended to no one else, make your confession in private, just between you and the one you sinned against. If you took some money from your father's wallet, you need not go to your neighbors and confess the theft to them. Confess it only to your father.

If you have sinned privately against someone, but your sin extended to others as well, make a private confession but include the others. If you manipulated your parents' last will and testament to cut your sister out so there would be more for you and your other siblings, you must confess your sin both to your sister and to your other siblings. But you need not confess it to your neighbor, who was not involved.

If you have sinned publicly against a group of people, make your confession publicly to all who have been affected by your sin. Suppose you stood up in church, condemned the pastor and the hypocrites in the church, and left in a huff—only to find out later that you had wronged them. Then you must return to the church, stand up again, confess your sin, and beg their forgiveness.

Always keep your confession to the smallest concentric circle. If you sinned against God alone, confess to God alone. If you sinned against God and your neighbor, confess to God and your neighbor. If you sinned against God, your neighbor, and the whole church, confess to God, your neighbor, and the whole church. Take your confession as far as it needs to go, but no further. Broadcasting your sin to the world doesn't help the world, and it certainly doesn't help you.

The good news about retracing your steps when you have failed to manage temptation is that this always takes you back to God. Since He is at that center concentric circle and since your sin is ultimately always directed at Him, by retracing your steps back through the people, places, and events that your sin has harmed, you will always make your way back to God. There He waits for you, always loving, ready to forgive and anxious to restore. Psalm 145:8 reminds us,

"The LORD is gracious and full of compassion, slow to anger and great in mercy." Comforting words for all of us.

Make restitution.

One aspect of repentance that we think little about—and would prefer to avoid altogether—is making restitution. In modern society, this is something of a lost art. The dictionary defines restitution as "a restoration of something to its rightful owner" or "a making good of or giving an equivalent for some injury."[1] The Bible has a lot more to say about it than does the dictionary.

I can hear the wheels turning in some heads now. "You mean, if I fall into temptation and sin, I not only have to confess that sin to all who are involved, but I have to make it right as well?" No, I'm not saying that…the Bible is.

The law of restitution

Leviticus 6 records the law of restitution. In essence it says, if something was delivered to you for safekeeping and you lost it, you would not only have to restore the lost item (or its value), but you would have to "add one-fifth more to it, and give it to whomever it belongs" (v. 5). If you stole something from your neighbor, you would have to give it back and add a 20 percent restitution penalty for having taken it in the first place.

Let's get specific. Suppose you stole a watch worth one hundred dollars from your local Wal-Mart. The Levitical law of restitution requires that you return that watch (or equivalent value if the watch was destroyed or lost) plus an additional 20 percent of the value. Your theft would result in a one hundred twenty dollar return on a one hundred dollar stolen watch. That's what restitution means. It's not a popular concept, but it's biblical, and it's right.

Numbers 5:5–7 says, "Then the LORD spoke to Moses, saying, 'Speak to the children of Israel: When a man or woman commits any sin that men commit in unfaithfulness against the LORD, and that person is guilty, then he shall confess the sin which he has committed. He shall make restitution for his trespass in full, plus one-fifth of it, and give it to the one he has wronged." It couldn't be plainer than that!

Zacchaeus and restitution

I anticipate your argument: "The passages you cited were from the Old Testament. That's the Levital law. The people in that time lived under the law; since Jesus came, we're under grace. Those old laws no longer apply." Sorry, but I can find no place in the New Testament where the law of restitution has been abrogated. In fact, a little story about a little man in the New Testament affirms the law of restitution.

When Zacchaeus climbed up into that sycamore tree to see Jesus and was seen by Jesus, God so convicted his heart that Zacchaeus was a changed man. He went up the tree a sinner, and he came down a sinner—but a changed sinner.

As the chief tax collector of Jericho (one of the three tax collection centers for the whole country—Caesarea and Capernaum being the other two), Zacchaeus was a rich man. Everyone knew the source of his wealth. Jewish tax collectors worked for the Roman government and paid dearly for the privilege. Once they won the contract to collect taxes and knew what their quota was, they could charge anything they wanted as markup to make their profit. Some tax collectors, like Zacchaeus, were exceptionally wealthy because they were exceptionally ruthless. Apparently this little guy was ruthless with a capital R.

When Jesus came into Zacchaeus's life and the tax collector was saved, he did a 180-degree about-face. He not only became exceptionally generous, giving half of his considerable goods to feed the poor (Luke 19:8), but he also determined that everything he had taken from the people, every denarius he had cheated out of them, would be returned. But more than that—and this is the amazing part—the money would not just be returned, but restoration would be made fourfold (v. 8). Don't let that escape your mind too quickly. For every denarius taken, four would be restored.

More than required

The Levitical law required a 20 percent penalty be added for restitution. In some cases, double restitution was made (Exodus 22:4, 7, 9). But fourfold? That was unheard of. To make restitution fourfold would have been unthinkable... unless, of course, a sinner had been gripped by the heinousness of his sin. For anyone who had not come to terms with the need to admit sin and be remorseful, restitution would be out of the question. Just how deeply must Zacchaeus have felt contrition and shame to make a fourfold restitution? That's when you know repentance is real.

You aren't required by God to make a fourfold restitution, but you may choose to do so, like Zacchaeus. Don't you think the God who is just in forgiving you of your sins (1 John 1:9) has a right to expect you to be just in restoring what you have taken?

Restitution, making things right, may not cost you a dime, but some form of restitution is always the best evidence that repentance has been real. Besides, restitution is the only way to get back to ground zero, to take the stone out of the pond and retract all the concentric circles. Any pain and hardship that restitution may cause cannot be compared with the pleasure of being fully restored to someone. It's always worth the effort.

LEARN FROM YOUR MISTAKES

Have you noticed how many people don't seem to learn anything from their mistakes? Some time ago there appeared an article in my local newspaper, the *Lincoln Journal Star,* about a scam artist arrested by the Lancaster County, Nebraska, Sheriff's Department. When a routine background check was run, they discovered that Harry Fowler had twenty-two known aliases, nine different claimed birth dates, and eight different social security numbers. His computerized "rap sheet" was more than eight feet long.[2] Apparently Harry was a slow learner (or a nonlearner).

The worst thing about making a mistake is failing to learn from it. Slipping into sin, stumbling and falling, staying down when you fall is always a painful experience. When Israel slipped away from God, He counseled His people to "ask for the old paths, where the good way is, and walk in it; then you will find rest for your souls" (Jeremiah 6:16). Getting back to the right path is a refreshing and rewarding experience, but it will last only if we learn from our errors. Here are some lessons we can learn from our mistakes.

It is impossible to successfully divert the blame for your sin.

While some people fail to learn from their mistakes, others do. Gordon MacDonald is one of them. Pastor of an innovative, vibrant evangelical church in New England, MacDonald fell into infidelity some years ago, and his ministry came to a grinding halt. But recognizing the foolishness of his sin and learning from his mistakes, he underwent a full program of restoration. Now, years later, he has returned to his church as pastor. His book *Rebuilding Your Broken World* is not an autobiography of his misbehavior or a study in self-pity. Instead, it is an account of how God can rebuild your broken world after you have destroyed it. MacDonald says:

> The broken-world person who lives with self-inflicted damage faces a heavy temptation to defend himself and his "territory." If he cannot escape responsibility for his misbehavior, he is tempted to do at least three things to ease the embarrassment. First, he is tempted to spread the blame for his deed. The mind sharpened by this pain of humiliation is adept at looking at all involved in the tragic events and trying to see what they did and did not do. Second, the person with the broken world may try to complain about how poorly he perceives he is being treated by his accusers and critics. And third, he is liable to diminish the seriousness of his own choices by concentrating on the sins of others. This way, he thinks, *I don't have to feel so badly about myself. They're as bad as I am.* Such thinking never brings rebuilding. It retards and usually defeats the process.[3]

MacDonald's excellent book has become a roadmap for those who have lost their way. But the best guide for returning from the dark night of sin is still God's Word.

It is impossible to hide sin successfully.

Adam and Eve tried it in the most idyllic environment in the world—the Garden of Eden. After they sinned against God, "They heard the sound of the LORD God walking in the garden in the cool of the day, and Adam and his wife hid themselves from the presence of the LORD God among the trees of the garden" (Genesis 3:8). They tried, but failed.

Moses tried it when he was angered at the way an Egyptian was treating a Hebrew slave. Exodus 2:12 says, "So he looked this way and that way, and when he saw no one, he killed the Egyptian and hid him in the sand." The very next day someone who had seen his angry act confronted him, and Moses had to flee to the backside of the desert for forty years. Moses tried, but failed.

Achan tried it when he took a beautiful Babylonian garment and some money from Jericho after the Israelites destroyed the city. God had forbidden the Jewish soldiers from taking any of the spoils of war. When confronted after the tragic defeat of Ai, Achan confessed, "When I saw among the spoils a beautiful Babylonian garment, two hundred shekels of silver, and a wedge of gold weighing fifty shekels, I coveted them and took them. And there they are, hidden in the earth in the midst of my tent, with the silver under it" (Joshua 7:21). Achan tried, but failed.

It is impossible to hide sin. David tried to hide his illicit act with Bathsheba by arranging Uriah's death, but still his sin was exposed. Judas tried to hide his sin by slithering up to the Savior in the darkness of the Garden of Gethsemane, but his sin will forever be known. Peter tried to hide his sin of cowardice, but when he denied the Lord the third time, the cock crowed, and it was all over.

Hebrews 4:13 says, "There is no creature hidden from His sight, but all things are naked and open to the eyes of Him to whom we must give account." If we ever learn this lesson, we'll save ourselves a lot of pain and grief.

It is impossible to prosper while you hide sin.

Some people have tried to hide their sin and have gotten away with it for a while. But as they were hiding their sin, their fortunes went south.

Proverbs 28:13 warns, "He who covers his sins will not prosper, but whoever confesses and forsakes them will have mercy." That sounds like a no-brainer of a plan. Confess and forsake sin, and you have all the mercy you want. Cover sin, and you have all the heartache you never wanted.

David understood this. He testified, "When I kept silent, my bones grew old through my groaning all the day long. For day and night Your hand was heavy upon me; my vitality was turned into the drought of summer" (Psalm 32:3–4). While David failed to own up to his sin and confess it, the hand of God lay heavy upon him. One military campaign after another met with only partial or no success. Enemy after enemy raised their voices and their spears against him. He silently held in his sin, but God was not so silent in bringing pressure to bear that would release David of that sin and ultimately bring forgiveness and restoration.

David continued, "I acknowledged my sin to You, and my iniquity I have not hidden. I said, 'I will confess my transgressions to the LORD,' and You forgave the iniquity of my sin" (v. 5). David's fortunes looked much brighter after he came clean with God. In fact, later in this same psalm he says, "Many sorrows shall be to the wicked; but he who trusts in the LORD, mercy shall surround him" (v. 10).

If you want to be blessed and prosper, be right before God. Get out in the open whatever it is you have done that has caused you to slip away from God. Admit it. Be remorseful about it. Confess it. Recognize that you did it against God, and ask Him to forgive and restore you. He will—you can count on it.

THE GOD OF THE SECOND CHANCE

If you're crumpled in a heap on the mat, defeated by Satan, suffering from spiritual vertigo and unable to get up, I have good news for you. No, I have *great* news for you. God is in your corner. He wants you to get up, and He's ready to help you up, revive you, and set you on your spiritual journey again. There is no sin so great that God's grace is not greater still. Nothing you have done is so horrible that you cannot experience God's forgiveness. All you have to do is follow the biblical directions outlined in this chapter.

If there is one great truth I have learned from my mistakes it is this: Our God is the God of the second chance. He is just, holy, and sovereign. God is not a pushover. But He is a parent, and as our heavenly Father He knows we will make mistakes. As a parent, He is ready—even eager—to forgive us and get us back on track.

The God of mercy

The Bible often speaks of God's mercy toward us. There are more than ample verses that attest to this. Think about these:

- "The LORD God [is] merciful and gracious, longsuffering, and abounding in goodness and truth" (Exodus 34:6).
- The LORD your God is a merciful God" (Deuteronomy 4:31).
- "The LORD is merciful and gracious, slow to anger, and abounding in mercy" (Psalm 103:8).

- "Return to the LORD your God, for He is gracious and merciful, slow to anger, and of great kindness" (Joel 2:13).
- "I know that You are a gracious and merciful God, slow to anger and abundant in lovingkindness" (Jonah 4:2).
- "'Return, backsliding Israel,' says the LORD; 'I will not cause My anger to fall on you. For I am merciful,' says the LORD; 'I will not remain angry forever'" (Jeremiah 3:12).
- "But you are God, ready to pardon, gracious and merciful, slow to anger, abundant in kindness" (Nehemiah 9:17).

It is God's character to be gracious, forgiving, merciful, and ready to pardon if we but confess our sins to Him. He wants to forgive you more than you want to be forgiven. That's His nature. He wants to make you useful again, and He knows that while you are bearing the burden of unconfessed sin, you cannot be of service to Him. God will not use a dirty vessel.

Few people appreciated God's willingness to grant second chances as much as Jonah. After hearing the clear call of God to go to Nineveh and preach a message of repentance, this wrong way prophet went to Joppa and bought a ticket for Tarshish, in the opposite direction from Nineveh. After a good dose of "whale-belly theology," Jonah got his act together, and God gave him a second chance. "Now the word of the LORD came to Jonah the second time" (Jonah 3:1). After an eight-word sermon, the whole city turned to God. Jonah's greatest ministry was after God had given Him a second chance. We can only guess how great his ministry would have been if he had taken God's first opportunity! But the second opportunity wasn't bad.

Ready to remold

One of the most tender verses in the Bible, a verse that I often use when someone says they've blown it so badly that God could never forgive them, is Jeremiah 18:1–4: "The word which came to Jeremiah from the LORD, saying: 'Arise and go down to the potter's house, and there I will cause you to hear My words.' Then I went down to the potter's house, and there he was, making something at the wheel. And the vessel that he made of clay was marred in the hand of the potter; so he made it again into another vessel, as it seemed good to the potter to make."

God is the potter; we are the clay. While the Potter was forming the clay on His wheel, He discovered something in the clay that caused it to be useless. It was marred. Maybe there was a speck of dirt in the clay or a mixture of iron or some other substance. Whatever it was, it caused the clay to be worthless. It was ruined. A human potter would have just thrown it out in the potter's field—but not God.

Our heavenly Potter once again shaped and molded the clay in a way that pleased Him. He gave it a second chance to be useful. He is the God of the second chance. He lifts us up, dusts us off, picks out the specks of dirt, and shapes us into a vessel fit for His use.

START OVER

One of the greatest secrets to success in the Christian life is learning to get up after you've fallen down. Sounds simple, doesn't it? But so many Christians today fail to rise when they fall to ruin. To be a champion, you've got to get up and start over no matter how many times you've blown it.

Dan Jansen must have thought he was jinxed. He was a world-class skater. Sure, he would fall occasionally, but very rarely—and not in a race, and certainly not in the Olympics. But he did. In fact, Dan Jansen fell twice in the 1988 Olympics and then again in the 1992 Olympics. In the 1994 Olympics, Jansen was predicted to win the men's five-hundred-meter event. But he didn't. On February 14, 1994, Jansen attempted to steady himself on a curve, and the friction caused by his hand simply touching the ice cost him the race. He finished a disappointing eighth.

A few days later, Dan Jansen took to the ice again, this time for the one-thousand-meter race. Things looked bleak. He had never won an Olympic race, even though he was often favored to do so. Seven skaters had already posted better times than Jansen's career best in the event. Nobody was encouraged. But Dan Jansen wouldn't quit. He laced up, took to the ice for what was not even "his" event, and promptly won the race in world-record time. After a decade of Olympic disappointment, starting over paid off for Dan Jansen.

Three threes

It was the day Peter would give half an eternity to live over. It was D day—denial day. His own personal day of tragedy.

Jesus was inching toward the cross. Everybody knew it. You could feel the tension mounting. Peter had boldly guaranteed that while the rest of the disciples might desert Jesus, he never would. Set the clock and listen to the ticking. It was only hours later that he denied the Lord three times, the final time with a curse (Matthew 26:69–75). Those gathered in the courtyard of Caiaphas were warming their hands, but it was their eyes that pierced Peter with blazing fire. He felt lower than a snake's belly. He had betrayed the Lord of Glory.

But in three days that same Lord would demonstrate Himself the Lord over death as well. Jesus rose from the dead, proving all the skeptics wrong. He lifted the heads of His discouraged disciples by giving them hope, but no head was lifted higher than Peter's, the one that had sunk the lowest. At the Sea of Galilee rendezvous site, Jesus suddenly appeared and ate breakfast with His disciples. After eating, the Savior turned to the defeated, deflated Peter and said, "Simon, son of Jonah, do you love Me?" (John 21:15–17). Three times Peter had denied the Lord; now, three times he reaffirmed his love for the Lord. It was as if Jesus was helping Peter start over, and it paid off.

Better than ever

The second half of Peter's ministry was much more astounding than the first half. Read the book of Acts. Peter became the principal preacher of Christianity after Jesus' resurrection and ascension into heaven. He was a pillar in the church of Jerusalem. So powerful was Peter's presence that people brought their sick out into the streets so they would be healed when Peter's shadow passed over them (Acts 5:15). Talk about a second chance!

It doesn't much matter what you've done in failing to manage temptation, you can reclaim territory Satan has taken from you. If you admit your sin, feel genuine remorse that leads to repentance, confess it as sin, and retrace your steps, making restitution if necessary; God will pick you up, dust you off, and let you start all over again.

In the hope that you will pick yourself up when you fall and start over, I pose one of the rare offerings from the small poet's corner of my mind.

When you've made your plans and they've gone awry,
When you've tried your best 'til there's no more try,
When you've failed yourself and you don't know why
START OVER.

When you've told your friends what you plan to do,
When you've trusted them but they didn't come through,
Now you're all alone and it's up to you
START OVER.

When you think you're finished and want to quit,
When you've bottomed out in life's deepest pit,
When you've tried and tried to get out of it
START OVER.

Starting over means victories won,
Starting over means a race well run,
Starting over means the Lord's 'Well done,'
...so don't just sit there, START OVER.

You can find the strength that brings success in Christian living, even if you've stumbled into sin. But you have to deal with sin appropriately. You have to deal with it purposefully. You have to deal with it biblically. If you fall, get up again. Start over and begin to enjoy success on your spiritual journey again.

SUCCESS SURVEY #6

1. *Have you failed to retake ground you lost to Satan because of sin?* If you are tempted to sin and you slip and fall, is your spiritual life over? Not at all. What if you are tempted and jump in with both feet? Is that the end? No. That's why God provided the 1 John 1:9 principle: "If we confess our sins, He is faithful and just to forgive us our sins and to cleanse us from all unrighteousness." Is it possible for you to retake the spiritual ground you lost when you failed to manage your temptation? It's not only possible, it's doable. Never give up!

2. *How easy is it for you to admit your sin?* Probably not very easy. And frankly, it's not supposed to be easy. It isn't easy for anyone, but it's necessary. Can you deal with your sin if you don't admit it? Not very well. So what is it in your life that you refuse to admit you have done? What is that one sin that keeps haranguing you and making you feel like a spiritual failure? Identify it. Admit it. Confess it. Get beyond it. That's spiritual progress.

3. *What do you need to confess today?* Have you ever heard people confessing sin that you didn't even know about? If you have, they likely didn't follow the "concentric circle pattern" of confession. So whom do you need to confess something to today? Are there others you're leaving out? Who else has been affected by your sin? Who needs to hear your confession? Now, beyond those affected, who needs to hear? No one. Keep it that way.

4. *Is it possible you need to do more?* If you have taken something from someone, whether it's their good name or their inheritance, isn't there something you yet need to do? The Bible often speaks about making restitution. Is there something you need to restore to someone before you can be a spiritual success? If the answer is yes (and you know it), what do you say? Are you willing to do the good work of restitution? Or are you willing to allow your spiritual growth to be impeded because you can't bring yourself to make restitution? The choice is yours. How badly do you want to be a success?

5. *What are the lessons you have learned from your mistakes?* Can you name them? Can you visualize them? Name a few, just to yourself. Have you benefited from what you've learned? In what ways? Name them. Have you enjoyed a second chance from God? If so, what did you do with it? Has it made a difference in your life?

KEEP YOUR EYE ON THE GOAL

We have all eternity to celebrate our victories,
but only one short hour before sunset in which to win them.
ROBERT MOFFAT

"Lay up for yourselves treasures in heaven."
MATTHEW 6:20

———❦———

O f the seven secrets to spiritual success, this one should be no secret to anyone. What a pity it's missed by so many Christians. In fact, sometimes it seems that God's people have made a collective, clandestine pact to keep this secret under wraps. After all, a large percentage of Christians live for the here and now, glancing only occasionally from this world to the next.

In *Alice in Wonderland,* when Alice came to a junction in the road that led in different directions, she asked the Cheshire Cat, "Cheshire-Puss…would you tell me please, which way I ought to go from here?"

"That depends a good deal on where you want to go to," said the Cat.

"I don't much care where," replied Alice.

"Then it doesn't matter which way you go."[1]

In the spiritual realm, keeping your eye on the goal means keeping your eye on eternity, and it matters a great deal which way you go.

Paul explained to the Roman Christians that salvation was not an afterthought with God, but was, in fact, the centerpiece of an eternal plan. The apostle used the five "golden links" of salvation's chain to explain that God was at work in eternity past, that He continues to work in the present, and that He will not finish the work of our salvation until eternity future. His exact words are found in Romans 8:29–30: "For whom He foreknew, He also predestined to be conformed to the image of His Son, that He might be the firstborn among many brethren. Moreover whom He predestined, these He also called; whom He called,

147

these He also justified; and whom He justified, these He also glorified."

Armed with this pan-eternal view of our salvation, we understand that part of the work of God in saving us took place long before time. In the distant eternal past, God foreknew and predestined us to be saved and thus ultimately to be conformed to the image of his Son. These two golden links were set in sovereign concrete before we were born.

Presently God is calling out from this world a people for His own, and those whom He calls He also justifies. These two golden links are being completed before our very eyes in the world today. What we haven't seen yet is the final link of the five—that's eternity future.

One day, those whom God foreknew and predestined in eternity past, those whom God is calling and justifying in eternity present, He will one day in eternity future glorify so we will be in every respect conformed to the image of His Son, Jesus Christ.

It is for this reason that we must keep our eye on eternity future. God isn't finished with us; there's much more to success in the Christian life than we see now. In fact, we won't really be successful until we are judged successful by Him after this life is over. The ultimate goal is still out there—in the future. Success in this life only comes to the extent that we keep our eye on the goal.

THIS WORLD IS NOT MY HOME

One of the popular television programs of the 1990s was *The X-Files*. The show's main characters were two FBI agents—Dana Scully, a pathologist with an analytical mind, and Fox Mulder, an extraterrestrial-oriented, paranormal-prone guy who was always chasing down those lost in the wonderful world of the weird. One reason the program garnered such a large following was because many people like to think about the possibility that creatures who have no earthly origin are indeed living in our midst. Could they be right? Read on.

I know of no more hopeless sounding passage in the Bible than Ephesians 2:12. Paul described what it was like for the Ephesian believers before they became Christians. Ephesus was one of the major cities of Asia Minor (modern Turkey) in the Roman world; thus, it was not a Jewish city. The believers in Ephesus were predominantly Gentiles. Paul said, "At that time you were without Christ, being *aliens* from the commonwealth of Israel and *strangers* from the covenants of promise, having no hope and without God in the world" (italics added).

Before these Ephesian Gentiles came to faith in Christ, they were aliens. Not aliens from outer space, of course, but alienated from the social life of Israel, total strangers to the benefits of God's covenants, hopeless with regard to any future and without God in the world. They might as well have been from another planet when it came to the things of God.

But all that changed one day. Hearing the gospel, they came to believe that Jesus Christ, and only He, could save them from their sins. They put their faith in what Jesus did on their behalf and trusted Him to be their Savior. They were made new creatures in Christ Jesus. They were no longer aliens to God.

New aliens

Then those Ephesians became aliens in a different way. No longer were they aliens from the benefits that God gives His chosen people, but in another sense, they were even more alienated than ever. Their hopes, dreams, and aspirations moved from the temporal to the eternal. Their goals became different from the other Ephesians around them. What was once important to them—turning a big profit in commerce, being a part of the social elite in their city, enjoying the nearby sea and mountains—was no longer foremost in their lives. They had become aliens, alienated from this world.

It's this way with you and me, too. Once our allegiances are transferred from earth to heaven, we know our earthly residence is temporary. When heaven becomes our destiny, it also becomes our goal; when it is our goal, all our energies are turned toward it. As G. K. Chesterton said, once heaven is our home, we will always be a little homesick until we get there. "The modern philosopher had told me again and again that I was in the right place, and I had still felt depressed even in acquiescence." But when Chesterton came to faith in Christ and knew "that I was in the wrong place...my soul sang for joy, like a bird in spring." He continues, "I knew now...why I could feel homesick for home."[2] When you're in the wrong place, nothing will do until you find your way to the right place.

When it comes to Christians, we often feel like that in this world, and we should. As the old song says, "This world is not my home; I'm just a-passin' though." We must never forget that.

A pilgrim mind-set

When you're a resident alien in a foreign country, it changes your approach to life. You are careful how deeply you drive down your stakes. You watch your conduct because you are not part of that society. That's also true when you are a spiritual alien in this world.

In Philippians, Paul describes us as citizens of heaven and says that because we're aliens here, we must let our "conduct be worthy of the gospel of Christ" (1:27). We must act and think differently because we are not of this world. We must adopt a pilgrim mind-set. We're moving on; we're not hanging around this old world.

In his book *Eternity*, Joe Stowell says the six characteristics of the pilgrim mind-set can be found by studying Hebrews 11:13–19. Briefly, the passage shows that as pilgrims:

(1) we live here believing God's promises will be fulfilled ultimately in the world to come (v. 13); (2) we readily sense we don't belong on earth, and are seeking the world to come (v. 13); (3) though we could choose to return and live in the earthbound environment from which we were called, we refuse to think backward to what is past (v. 15); (4) we believe nothing here compares to the better country to which we are going, so our affections are set there (v. 15); (5) with our affections on eternity, God is not ashamed to be called our God (v. 15); (6) nothing here is of greater value than our relationship with God, therefore we can be obedient to the point of ultimate sacrifice (vv. 17–19).[3]

No earthly good

Often when I talk about living in light of eternity, some (even Christians) ask, "Don't you think that if you do that you'll be so heavenly minded you'll be no earthly good?" I counter with what has been my honest observation in life. In more than fifty years as a Christian, I have never yet met a Christian who was so heavenly minded he was no earthly good. But I have met thousands upon thousands of Christians who were so earthly minded they were no heavenly good.

Phil was an investment broker for a major firm. He and three friends began meeting with Derrick, a former pastor and conference speaker, in a discipleship group. While all four met faithfully and grew for six months, Phil's interest began to wane after that. His friends continued to encourage him, but he always seemed to have an excuse: "Meeting with a major client." "Have to get these reports done." "Can't afford to turn down this opportunity for a deal." "Gotta put in extra hours this week—duty calls." The problem was, as Phil's friend Gary ultimately observed, "He had become so focused on earthly riches that he forgot about eternal rewards."

Let's not be fooled by the pop philosophy of being too heavenly minded. When you're saved and on your way to eternity with God, it's impossible to be too heavenly minded. Of course we can live as though the present doesn't matter, and that's a colossal mistake. C. S. Lewis observed in his book *Mere Christianity*, "Aim at heaven and you'll get earth thrown in. Aim at earth and you'll get neither."[4] I wish I'd said that!

The secret to spiritual success now is to view this world as a passageway from eternity past to eternity future. Fail to see that you're just "a-passin' through," and you'll fail to realize the rest of that old gospel song: "My treasures are laid up, somewhere beyond the blue." But how will you keep this eternal perspective on daily life in Dullsville? How can you live fruitfully today based on the promise of tomorrow? Here's a little spiritual secret I learned early in my Christian life.

BEGIN EVERY DAY AT THE JUDGMENT SEAT

More than twenty years of my life were spent as a teacher. I loved it. The years of ministry I've spent out of the classroom have been wonderful, but to some degree I have missed the interaction with students every day I've been away from the classroom.

I remember distinctly the day back in 1973 when one of my students asked me a question about the judgment seat of Christ. I answered his question to his satisfaction…but not to mine. I went to our college library to seek additional help, but to my amazement there were almost no books written on the subject of the judgment seat. My faculty colleagues encouraged me to write one. Thus, with a book originally entitled *It Will Be Worth It All,* first published in 1977, my writing ministry was launched.

(Since it was my first book, I thought it appropriate to dedicate it to my wife. I said, "Dedicated to my beloved wife LINDA whose encouragement has meant so much to me in the study of God's Word." I only mention this because many years later the publisher decided to change the cover design and title. So the book is now titled *Tested by Fire,* which fuels speculation about why it's dedicated to my wife! I thought I had better explain.)

The first chapter of this book is called "It's Too Late Now." I wanted to paint a portrait of what it might be like when the Lord comes, and all opportunity to serve Him this side of heaven is gone forever. I quote an extended portion of that first chapter scenario:

Who was really ready? None of us! We had been waiting for this day, we had sung about it, read about it, longingly anticipated it; but when it finally came, we were caught completely off guard. There was so much more to be done. We had so many good intentions, so many good plans. There were meetings to be held, campaigns and programs to be organized. Our visitation committee was just coming alive. We were in the middle of planning our annual fall evangelistic crusade at the church. We had so much potential for future service to the Lord. Now, all those plans, those preparations and programs, all that potential is meaningless.

I know this should be the happiest day of my life, but these thoughts keep darting through my mind. Oh sure, the instant it happened, my mind was overrun with what I had just seen. To think that after years of anticipation and anxious waiting, we now have actually experienced the Lord's return! I am with Him! He really did come back, as He said He would.

How vivid my memory is of that split second ago when I heard the shrill yet melodious blast of the trumpet. The sweetest voice ever heard triumphantly called me to come up to Him. Jesus Christ has returned and now time is swallowed up in the present of eternity. All these miraculous things have taken place before you could bat an eyelash, and I was astonished by them.

Yet, with so much to think about, my mind still reverts to the gigantic amount of service I've left behind. Trying to tell myself not to worry about it, or even think about it, just doesn't work. What I could have done for the Lord, and did not do, will never get done. I just can't seem to put this out of my mind.

I keep asking myself, "Why didn't I do more when I had the chance? What was the matter with me?" I knew better. I was well aware of the Lord's command. He was depending on me. Why did I spend so much time on foolish things? Why didn't I spend more time telling others of the hope I had? How could I have allowed my service to the Lord to be so minimal?

But now all this questioning is useless. Now I can't share the Lord's love with others. "Forgive me. Please forgive me, Lord Jesus, for not taking my responsibility as a Christian more seriously when I could do something about it. Forgive me, for it's too late now!"[5]

Start there and work backward.

It was upon writing these words in 1973 that I decided I needed to begin every day at the judgment seat. After all, if everything we enjoy for all eternity is awarded at the judgment seat of Christ, shouldn't we know now what the Lord is looking for in our lives, rather than wait until then, when it's too late? Makes sense to me. So every day I start there and work backward.

Each morning I pray and ask the Lord to help me do everything that day so it will be judged acceptable at the judgment seat. I ask Him to help me live with the judgment seat in mind. I submit my plans for the day, my appointments, my mind, my body, my all to Him. I ask Him to flash my moment before the judgment seat across my mind as I make my way through the day. By doing this, I can apply what the Lord is looking for then to what I am doing now.

Over the years, others have implemented a similar tactic in other areas of life. For example, in reading Stephen Covey's phenomenal best-seller *The 7 Habits of Highly Effective People,* the second habit is "Begin with the End in Mind." Covey comments, "To begin with the end in mind means to start with a clear understanding of your destination. It means to know where you're going so that you better understand where you are now and so that the steps you take are always in the right direction."[6]

The guideline grid

As a Christian, my past is blotted out by the shadow of Calvary's cross. My future is also hidden in this emblem of God's love. But my future reward is not determined at the cross but at the judgment seat of Christ. That's why I must live every moment of my life in light of that event, because every moment is judged by that event. Any success you and I enjoy in life will be determined as success only at the judgment seat. Until then, we must live with the guideline grid of that day laid over our lives. That grid includes:

- serving the Lord faithfully, the basic requirement of a steward (1 Corinthians 4:2);
- serving the Lord with the proper motives, because even the secret counsels of our heart will be revealed at that day (1 Corinthians 4:5);
- serving the Lord to the fullness of our potential, for each of us is given different abilities from the Lord (Luke 12:48);
- serving the Lord in accordance with our opportunities, for not all are given the same occasions to serve Him (Matthew 20:1–16);
- serving the Lord by letting Him work through us, because only as He works through us is it rewardable work; work done in our own strength is unrewardable (Galatians 2:20).

Only by taking what the Word teaches us about the judgment seat of Christ, and what the righteous Judge will be looking for on that day, can we know that we are living in a way that has the potential of success.[7]

KEEP FIRST THINGS FIRST

When you keep your eye on the goal of eternity, it not only changes the way you do things, but it also changes the way you view things. Among the core changes those living with eternal focus will experience are these:

People are more important than programs.

If you take a look at the millions of dollars being spent by churches on gigantic sanctuaries that are used only a few hours a week, church weight rooms constructed so members can pump iron and witness to unbelievers at the same time, and the latest computerized state-of-the-art equipment, you might wonder how the first-century church got along without all this stuff. Well, times change; needs change. And, of course, you need facilities in order to function—nice facilities. But is it possible that even the church has failed to keep its eye on the goal? Are we spending too much on programs and facilities and seeing too little in the way of changed lives? Are we getting a poor "return" on our investment?

Jesus constantly elevated the value of people. He stooped to pick up those who fell at His feet. He healed the lame and gave sight to the blind. He fed the hungry. He gave hope to the downtrodden. He ate with sinners and outcasts. He treated a woman who had had five husbands with uncommon respect. He came "to seek and to save that which was lost" (Luke 19:10). Jesus kept His eye on the goal.

When people came to Jesus, they went away changed. He was in the business of changing lives. As far as I can determine from reading my Bible, the rich young man who came to Jesus asking what he must do to inherit eternal life is the only person in the Bible who came seriously seeking Jesus and went away unhappy (Mark 10:17–22). All others who genuinely wanted Jesus to change their lives were changed.

With eternal focus we see people differently. They are not numbers, statistics, or percentages reflected in a poll. They are people who need a Savior. They are no longer a commodity but creatures who need the saving grace of God. We no longer see our neighbors as either people to enjoy or problems to endure; we see them as souls on their way either to heaven or hell.

We look at our families differently, too. We respond to them with genuine love and appreciation—not just because they are family, but because they are eternal creations of God. When we keep our eye on the goal, the hordes at a football game are not just fans—they are candidates for heaven. People become important, genuinely of eternal import.

Purity is more important than popularity.

Is there anything as fleeting as fame? Popularity just doesn't last. Take Winston Churchill, for example. A few years ago, the *San Francisco Examiner* reported that one-third of all British children had never heard of him. Some thought this famous leader was an American president. Others said he was a songwriter. This is the man of whom the *Observer* newspaper wrote in 1951: "In a thousand years from now, his name will be popularly known; it will conjure up a warm glow, a proud smile, and signify what is most bold and generous in human nature." And to this today's British youth are asking, "Winston who?"[8]

Our American heroes are not exempt from the flight of fame either. In 1991, Miami Dolphin coach Don Shula took a post-season trip to a small seaside town in Maine. He wanted to relax and "get away from it all" in delightful anonymity. It was raining when he and his wife arrived, so they decided to take in a movie. Well, guess what. When they entered the theater, the handful of people there broke into applause. After they were seated, Don said to his wife, "I guess there's nowhere I'm not known." A man seated nearby reached over and shook Shula's hand. Shula said, "I have to admit I'm kind of surprised that you know me here." The man replied, "Should I know you? We're just happy to see you folks, because the manager said he wasn't going to start the movie until at least two more people showed up."[9]

While popularity is fleeting, purity is forever. And purity is far more important than popularity. And while popularity and purity are not mutually exclusive, they often don't seem to run on parallel tracks. When they don't, hard choices have to be made.

The choice is clear for those who have learned the seventh secret to spiritual success. We understand that what we do in this life is grooming for the next. Grooming for eternity takes on a whole new meaning when we remember that Christ is the Bridegroom and we are His bride.

No one at a wedding is as pretty as the bride. She wears the beautiful white gown. Everyone stands when she makes her way down the aisle. All eyes are on her. Her groom beams with pride and grins broadly. This is her day. She is lovely. But suppose the bride was careless on the way to the wedding. Suppose she waded through a mud puddle as she walked to the church and then stumbled into a hedge. Her dress is now a mess and her hair a fright. The wedding is to begin momentarily, and there's no time to change. As she makes her way down the aisle, the audience politely stands, turns to the bride…and collectively gasps at what they see. The groom looks at her, sees her disheveled hair and soiled gown, and his proud grin fades. Everyone is horrified.

You and I are on the way to our wedding—the marriage supper of the Lamb—where we will be joined to our Bridegroom forever. We don't know the day nor the hour when the Groom will call us, but we do know it could be at anytime. Living in light of this eternal certainty should change the way we take care of ourselves. The apostle John encourages his readers with these words: "And it has not yet been revealed what we shall be, but we know that when He is revealed, we shall be like Him, for we shall see Him as He is. And everyone who has this hope in Him purifies himself, just as He is pure" (1 John 3:2–3).

If today you face the choice between popularity and purity, remember whose bride you are and how soon the wedding may take place. For the Christian looking for the secrets to spiritual success, purity is not just a distant hope, but a present reality. Remind yourself each morning that the answer to the question, "Who may ascend into the hill of the LORD? Or who may stand in His holy place?" is and always has been, "He who has clean hands and a pure heart" (Psalm 24:3–4).

You don't have to be popular to be spiritually successful, but you do have to be pure. Horace Greeley was right: "Fame is vapor, popularity an accident, riches take wings. Only one thing endures, and that is character." Keep the first things first. "Keep yourself pure" (1 Timothy 5:22).

Eternal success is more important than temporal success.

Try to put yourself in Jesus' place. People were more important to Him than programs or temples or positions. He wasn't always popular, but He was always pure. His success on earth was limited. Sure, He gathered a following, most of whom thought He would oust the Romans and establish Jewish dominance in Israel again. A few, undoubtedly, were looking for more miracles or more loaves and fishes. But while His temporal success was limited, His eternal success was limitless. He paid the penalty for the sins of mankind and opened the door to an eternity in heaven with God.

In some respects, everyone who finds Jesus finds eternal success. Just to know Him personally, intimately, in a saving way, secures eternal success for us. But there's so much more to heaven than just getting in. Keep your eye on the goal so you are not detained by the momentary thrill of temporal success but are driven by the crowning joy of eternal success.

I want you to meet some people who kept their eye on the goal.

At age sixteen, C. T. Studd was already an expert cricket player, and at nineteen he was made captain of his team at Eton, one of the elite schools in England. Soon he became a world famous sports personality. But the Lord had different plans for him.

While attending Cambridge University, C. T. Studd heard D. L. Moody preach and was wondrously converted. His eyes became fixed on the goal of eternity. Soon he dedicated himself, his life, his future, and his fortunes to the Lord. He spent hours trying to convert his teammates. Sensing God's leading, he offered himself to Hudson Taylor for missionary work in China.

While in China, Studd inherited a significant sum of money, equivalent to more than half a million dollars today. He was set for life. But with the seventh secret to spiritual success firmly fixed in his mind, Studd gave his entire inheritance away within twenty-four hours, investing in various works for the Lord. Eventually he was forced to go back to England because of ill health, but when he recovered, he returned to the mission field, this time to Africa. He was warned that if he went he would not live long. But temporal success meant little to C. T. Studd. He served the Lord in Africa until God called him home.

Paul P. Tell Sr. was one of the wealthiest men I knew personally. But that's not why I loved him; he was also one of the godliest men I ever knew. Paul was a brilliant businessman who lived in Akron, Ohio. He had a gift for knowing when to make a deal, when to move ahead, and when to wait. God richly blessed Paul, his dear wife, Anne, and their family.

When Paul P. Tell Sr. died on the eve of Father's Day 1997, he was eighty-three. Paul was my encourager, mentor, and friend. We know the man from

Tarsus as Paul the apostle; I knew this man from Akron as Paul the partner, and so did many others. Paul Tell was a philanthropist as well as a businessman. He wanted to communicate the gospel to every nation, and he partnered with many of God's people to accomplish this goal.

Four words characterized Paul Tell's life. Live. Christ. Die. Gain. The verse he lived by and finally died by was Philippians 1:21, "For to me, to live is Christ, and to die is gain." Paul Tell would never be a missionary to China or Africa as was C. T. Studd. But he made sure others could. In 1952, Paul and Anne Tell began a small foundation with the continuing goal of taking to the world the good news that Jesus saves. Paul knew how to spot a good investment—and for him, the best investment was an eternal investment.

Paul Tell Sr. read through his Bible each year. Every time I talked with him he could hardly wait to tell me what he had read that day. Paul was a faithful witness for his Lord and led many people to the Savior. But what I remember most about him was his boundless energy, his exuberant optimism, and his single-mindedness. Perhaps more than anyone else, he taught me that it will be worth it all when we see Christ.

If you've seen the film Chariots of Fire, you may think you know the story of Eric Liddell, but you only know half of it. The young Scottish ministerial student was the best sprinter in the British Isles and was favored to win the hundred-meter event at the 1924 Olympics in Paris. But when he learned that the preliminary race was to be held on a Sunday, his religious convictions prohibited him from participating.

Even though the hundred meters was his event, he spent the next several weeks training for another event that was not to be held on Sunday. On the closing day of the Olympics, he stood on the winner's platform and graciously received the gold medal in the four-hundred-meter event. Eric Liddell was hailed as a champion, the consummate success in this world. But that's not the end of the story.

In 1925, to the dismay of the athletic world, he returned to China under the London Missionary Society to teach at the Anglo-Chinese Christian College. When the Japanese overran China during World War II, Eric Liddell and his colleagues were taken to a concentration camp. There, from 1942 until his death in 1945, Eric Liddell was faithful in encouraging those interned with him and reaching out to those who would be his enemy. Scotland's greatest athlete could not settle for temporal success because he had learned the seventh secret to spiritual success.

—◦◈◦—

I will never hear the name Jim Elliot without thinking of his four brave colleagues—Nate Saint, Pete Fleming, Roger Youderian, and Ed McCulley. Jim's
story is their story.

Jim Elliot was a gifted writer and speaker and had a commanding presence
while a student at Wheaton College. He was a champion wrestler. He had the
world by the tail and distinguished himself in any endeavor he wanted. But he
couldn't shake the reality that this life was short and eternity was very long. While
a Wheaton student he wrote: "[God makes] His ministers a flame of fire. Am I
ignitable? God deliver me from the dread asbestos of 'other things.'"

In the winter of 1952, Elliot set sail on a freighter for Ecuador, where he
would work among the Aucas, an unreached Indian tribe. There he joined forces
with his four faithful friends. In the autumn of 1955, missionary pilot Nate Saint
spotted an Auca village. During the ensuing months, the five men dropped gifts
from a plane, attempting to befriend the hostile tribe. In January 1956, the five
missionaries landed on a beach of the Curaray River in eastern Ecuador. They had
left behind all hopes of conquering this world. Their eyes were fastened on a big-
ger goal.

They had several friendly contacts with the fierce tribe that had previously
killed several Shell Oil Company employees. But on January 8, 1956, all five men
were speared and hacked to death by the warriors from the Auca tribe. It was
their blood that opened the door to a thriving Auca church today. Though their
lives were cut short, Jim Elliot and his friends were eternally successful.

—◦◈◦—

You may not recognize the name Bryan Kroll, other than the fact that his surname
is the same as mine. Bryan was my nephew and an inspiration to my family and
many others.

Bryan Gerald Kroll was born in 1967 on his great-grandfather's birthday,
February 22, to my brother and sister-in-law, Jerry and Linda Kroll. Six weeks
after Bryan was born, the doctors diagnosed him with hemophilia. Bryan had
zero clotting factor in his blood. The physicians cautioned my brother and sister-
in-law that Bryan probably would not live to adulthood. But God had a better
idea. God gave Bryan to Jerry and Linda for twenty years.

Bryan never allowed his condition to hamper his life. He had to have frequent injections of clotting factor in order to inhibit unprecipitated bleeding, but
he would play like any normal kid. He and my son, Tim, were only three months
apart in age and were inseparable—best friends. When Bryan was a senior in
high school and was making plans for college, he became strangely sick. Things

just weren't right. He began to experience unexplainable internal pain. Doctors ran test after test to diagnose Bryan's condition. Finally they called my brother and sister-in-law in for a consultation. Because the frequent injections of clotting factor were harvested from blood that was not screened in those days, Bryan was diagnosed as HIV positive. Shortly, Bryan's miracle life would be ended by the plague of the twentieth century—AIDS.

While Bryan lay in intensive care at the Virginia Medical College hospital, struggling in his last days of life, he motioned to his mother and father that he wanted a pad to write on. What he wrote proved that he both lived and died with eternity in view: "Give everything I have to Jesus." His final request was for his mom and dad to take his life savings—about two hundred dollars—and invest it in the Lord's work.

Bryan was not a pastor, missionary, or wealthy philanthropist. He had little time on this earth, but he used that time well. He never took his eye off the goal.

And the beat goes on. Those who have learned the secrets to spiritual success live for eternal reasons. They sacrifice the potential of time for the marvel of eternity. They know this world is not their home; they're just a-passin' through. Their treasures are laid up somewhere beyond the blue. When spiritually successful Christians fall on the battlefield, they are replaced by others who have their eye on heaven.

Been there, done that.

Keeping your eye on the goal is a whole lot easier on paper than it is in real life. But we don't live on paper. With car payments to make, diapers to change, meals to deliver to your aging mother, and college tuition to pay, the everyday press of life has the strong potential of shifting our focus from eternal things to temporal things. It's one thing to know you should live with eternity in mind, it's another thing to do it when you're hurrying to get the kids dressed for school. I remember hearing Ed Dayton say, "The cleanliness of theory is no match for the mess of reality." How true.

God always brings some defining moment during the mundane of our lives to help us know if we are living with eternity in view. For my wife and me, it happened twice.

I was the chairman of the Division of Religion at Liberty University in Lynchburg, Virginia, during the 1970s. It was a responsibility I cherished. Having a positive influence on hundreds of students was extremely fulfilling. Linda and I thought we would be there forever, so in 1979 we bought some property on the top of a mountain and built a house. It was our dream home. It was much more than we deserved, so the day we moved in, we knelt by our bed and gave the house to the Lord. We held hands and prayed, "Lord, this is your house. We'll have Joy clubs, Five-Day clubs, backyard VBS, anything you ask. We want this house to be a witness to our community. And, Lord, if you choose, you may take this house from us at any time."

You have to be careful when you tell the Lord that He may take something whenever He wants it. Just fifteen months later, without any warning, the college I had taught at years earlier asked if I would consider returning to become its president. We really didn't want to go; we had just built our house. But we became convinced that the Lord wanted us there, so we put our dream home on the market and moved to New York State to take up our responsibilities at Practical Bible College. We turned the key on the lock, took one last look, and left our empty house.

We just walked away from the most expensive possession we had. We committed it to God's care and left it behind. We were sure a beautiful new house like that would sell in no time, but it didn't. In fact, it took three years and three months for that house to sell. It was as if God was saying to us, "Let's see if you really trust me. Let's see if your possessions in this life mean more to you than eternity does."

I served Practical Bible College as president for ten years. God was good to us. He significantly blessed the college while we were there. But in January 1990, God made me restless. I hadn't been open to considering another position for a decade, but now I wasn't sure what God was doing. Looking back, of course, I know. He was causing this restlessness so I would be willing to go when *Back to the Bible* invited me to become president and Bible teacher. By August 1990, we had packed up the truck and placed our New York house on the market, again thinking it would sell in no time. How well I remember a little conversation I had with God. I said, "Lord, you know that lesson you wanted to teach me when our Virginia house didn't sell for three years and three months? Well, I'm sure I learned it."

But again I had to trust God and lift my eyes from time to eternity. And once again God was checking to see which meant more to us, our house or our obedience to Him. For the second time we locked the door to our most expensive of worldly goods and simply walked away. I can tell you that this time it did not take three years and three months to sell the house. No, this time it took three years and four months. The real estate market in that part of the country was so flat that we lost a bundle of money on the sale of that house.

And do you know what? I'd do it all again in a split second. I have discovered that when I hold all my worldly possessions up against one moment of eternity, there is no comparison. I can walk away from anything! It has been one of the most liberating, most blessed lessons God has taught me on my own spiritual journey. God never asks us to give up anything we really need. He only asks us to live for something more than the things of time.

So how are you doing?

Are you keeping your eye on the goal? Do you begin each day at the judgment seat of Christ and work backward? Is the tyranny of the urgent destroying your ability to focus on what's really important, the timelessness of eternity? Be honest.

If you're not satisfied with the impact that eternity is having on your "now," here are some practical things you can do.

1. Begin by setting aside time today to talk with God about it. Clear your schedule. Don't answer the door during this time. Let the phone ring. Give God the time He deserves, and you deserve, to do some eternal business.

Do this in solitude. Go into a room, shut the door, and wait. When you sense God is there to meet with you, pour out your heart to Him. Talk out loud if you want. Get things right with Him. Tell Him what's bugging you about your life and your attitudes toward eternity. Confess your sin to Him. Clear the slate. Ask Him to help you leave that room with clean hands and a pure heart so your future can be much more successful than your past has been. Get ready for God to make changes in you.

2. To see the importance of eternity more clearly, write a personal mission statement. Steven Covey suggests this as part of the seven habits of highly effective people. "The most effective way I know to begin with the end in mind is to develop a personal mission statement or philosophy or creed. It focuses on what you want to be [character] and to do [contributions and achievements] and on the values or principles upon which being and doing are based."[10]

Keep your personal mission statement simple, such as: "I want to glorify God in every area of my life and live with eternity in view so that everything I am and everything I do will have eternal significance." You can then flesh out your statement by addressing various areas of life and how you plan to reflect glory to God in those areas. Work from the general to the specific. The benefit of this exercise is that it gives you a written statement to hold you accountable. When you fail in a given area, you know because your actions do not match your stated intentions.

3. To do things that have eternal impact, make a list of what you want to accomplish before you die. When people come to me for advice on how to get things done, I always ask them, "What's the last thing you want to do before you die?" To date, I've never had an answer. You see, knowing the last thing you want to do before you die is important. It will have an impact on what you do today, for today you may do the last thing you do before you die.

In their popular book *Chicken Soup for the Soul,* Jack Canfield and Mark Hansen tell the story of John Goddard. At age fifteen, Goddard sat at the kitchen table of his Los Angeles home and began compiling what he called "My Life List." On this list he placed 127 things he wanted to do or accomplish in his life. Since that time he has completed 108. These goals weren't trivial—they were big things of a lifetime. They included climbing the world's major mountains, exploring vast waterways (such as the Amazon, Congo, and Nile Rivers), running a mile in five minutes, reading the complete works of Shakespeare, and (believe it or not) reading the entire *Encyclopaedia Britannica.*[11]

You know why a lot of us come to old age and feel we haven't accomplished much? Because we don't know what it is that we want to accomplish. Be like Santa Claus. Make a list and check it twice. And make sure the items on your list reflect that you have your eye on the goal.

4. Honestly assess the eternal value of what you want to do. Often we put things on our list like "Visit Paris" or "Write a novel." While these may be personally satisfying, are they eternally rewarding? Can a person who has tapped into the seven secrets to spiritual success really find happiness in accomplishing the goals of this world? Can the world deliver on the promises it has made to us? I don't think so and neither did C. S. Lewis.

Lewis remarked, "Most people, if they had really learned to look into their own hearts, would know that they do want, and want acutely, something that cannot be had in this world. There are all sorts of things in this world that offer to give it to you, but they never quite keep their promise."[12]

You alone can make yourself feel good about what you have done with your life, and you don't have to wait until the judgment seat if you live with your eye on the goal. Enjoy living in this beautiful world, but don't be fooled. The best is yet to come.

5. Put the big rocks in first. Though I can't attest to the validity of the following story, it made quite an impression on me. Perhaps better than any other, it illustrates what I mean by keeping your eye on the goal.

One day a time-management expert, speaking to a group of business students, set a one-gallon, wide-mouthed glass jar on a table in front of him. Then he produced a half dozen fist-sized rocks and carefully placed them, one at a time, into the jar. When the jar was filled to the top, he asked, "Is this jar full?"

Everyone in the class said, "Yes."

He replied, "Really?" and reached under the table to pull out a bucket of gravel. Once he dumped some gravel in and shook the jar to allow the gravel to work its way down into the spaces between the big rocks, he again asked, "Is the jar full?"

By this time the class was suspicious. "Probably not," one student answered.

"Good!" he replied. He reached under the table and brought out a bucket of sand. After he dumped the sand into the jar and it sifted into all the spaces left between the rocks and the gravel, again the expert asked, "Is this jar full?"

"No!" the class shouted.

"Good!" he said. Then he grabbed a pitcher of water and began to pour it in until the jar was filled to the brim. Finally, the jar was full.

Then the man looked up at the class and asked, "What is the point of this illustration?"

One eager beaver raised his hand and said, "The point is, no matter how full your schedule is, if you try really hard, you can always fit some more things into it!"

"No," the speaker replied, "that's not it. The point is that if you don't put the big rocks in first, you won't get them in at all."

Keeping first things first will daily cause you to deal with the big rocks in your life—your relationship with God, your family, your church, your neighborhood, your colleagues. The big rocks are always those that touch eternity. You can best tell how you're doing in keeping your eye on the goal if you keep your hands on the big rocks of life.

So how will you know? How will handling the big rocks be evident to you? Easy.

Look at the stubs on your checkbook. See if you're spending what God entrusts to you on eternal things or temporal things. See if you've been buying a lot of sand and water or investing in big rocks.

Take a look at your calendar. Are your days and evenings a prelude to eternity, or are they tied up by the tentacles of time? How are you spending your time?

It's not hard to see how we're doing if we take an honest look. What's hard is mustering the honesty to measure the size of the rocks.

Keep your eye on the goal. Live for eternity. And don't ever lose the significance of that oft-used but undeniably true maxim: "Only one life 'twill soon be past; only what's done for Christ will last."

SUCCESS SURVEY #7

1. *Do you ever feel out of place in this world?* If you are making good progress on your spiritual journey, do you occasionally feel a little like an alien? Does it sometimes seem like you are a fish swimming upstream? A square peg in a round hole? A brown shoe at a formal occasion? You get the picture. For the Christian whose feet are in this world but whose heart is already in heaven, we sometimes feel like aliens in this world, and we should. So how do you feel? Are you too comfortable here to be homesick for heaven? Do you have your eye on the goal?

2. *What do you know about the judgment seat of Christ?* Are you aware that everything you retain and enjoy for all eternity is awarded as a result of His findings at the judgment seat? Do you know what He's looking for from you? If you don't, wouldn't it be a good idea to find out now before it's too late?

3. *What is the most important thing in your life?* Are you investing all your time, energies, talents, and money in this life? Are you living as if this is all there is? What are the first things in your life? What do you wake up thinking about each morning? And what do you go to bed thinking about each night? If programs are more important to you than people, if popularity is more important than purity, how will you account for that at the judgment seat?

4. *If you need to make some changes in your life in order to be spiritually successful, where will you start?* How about starting with your relationship with God? Do you have a special time and place you meet Him each day? Are your days filled with eternal realities or just temporal pleasures? Whatever is done for time lasts just for today. Whatever is done for God lasts for eternity. Which has occupied most of your day today?

5. *What are the big rocks in your life?* Lay them all out before you. The big rocks of your life. The gravel. The sand. And the water. Take a good look at them. Take the time to identify everything in your life and classify it. There will be lots of sand and water, and even a good supply of gravel. But the big rocks? They are very few. Are you keeping your eye on the goal? You can answer all the questions on your spiritual survey and feel pretty good about yourself, but if you can't identify your big rocks, you may be filling your jar with unimportant grains of sand. Spiritual success is learning how to live in such a way as to prosper in godly things. So how are you doing, really?

SATAN'S ATTEMPT TO STEAL
OUR SECRETS

L ike the U.S. and the Soviet Union during the Cold War, we are engaged in
a battle of stealth with our spiritual enemy. Satan would like nothing more
than to steal our spiritual secrets just like a spy wants to pilfer intelligence
secrets. And Satan is good at what he does. He is quite successful at blocking our
spiritual journey by stealing the impact—if not the reality—of our secrets to spiritual success. He often does this by getting us sidetracked or causing us to spin
our wheels. We soon discover what may be on the journey, but we are not making progress.

The late Vance Havner, a skillful preacher and wordsmith from the hills of
western North Carolina, used to say, "How long you've been a Christian only tells
how long you've been on the road. It doesn't tell how far you've come."

Are you one of those Christians who have been on the road quite a while, but
you aren't too thrilled with your progress? It doesn't take much for Satan to
thwart spiritual advancement, and he has a bag of tricks that outlasts Harry
Houdini, David Copperfield, and the Great Kreskin combined. Which of the
devil's devices is most effective on you?

In 7 Secrets to Spiritual Success, we have reflected on some of the spiritual pot-
holes on our journey, the ones Satan most often uses to slow our progress. Satan
will do anything to keep sinners from trusting Jesus Christ as Savior. He can't, of
course, but he will try. Once we have trusted Christ, the battles aren't over, but
the victory is assured. Jesus said ever so clearly and decisively, "And I give them

eternal life, and they shall never perish; neither shall anyone snatch them out of My hand. My Father, who has given them to Me, is greater than all; and no one is able to snatch them out of My Father's hand" (John 10:28–29).

When Satan fails to keep us from believing the gospel and coming to Christ, he does not give up on us. He just shifts his strategy. The outcome of the war is certain, but spiritual battles rage daily.

Satan tried tempting Pete with sex. A businessman who traveled constantly for a company in Lincoln, Nebraska, Pete was always encountering willing women in hotels and at business conventions. Yet Pete maintained his moral integrity by saying no the way Joseph did in the Old Testament. After a while it seemed Satan changed his approach, and Pete experienced greater financial success than he had ever had. Before long, his spiritual sensitivity began to decline as the money and prestige of his position became the most important thing in this life.

That's what Satan does. He never gives up on us; if one tactic doesn't work, he just tries another. He is like a college football team that doesn't stand a chance of winning a national championship but could play the role of spoiler for a team that could become champion. Satan can't keep us from heaven, but he can spoil our spiritual life on this side of death and our opportunity for reward on the other side. And how does he do that? Seven words describe his tactics.

DOUBT

Since Satan cannot keep us from salvation, he'll try to make us live in a constant, paralyzing fear that we are not saved. He'll whisper in our ear things like, "You can't be saved and have those thoughts" or "Do you think a saved person would get angry like that?" Satan is good at planting doubt. That's what he did to ruin Eve (Genesis 3:1). Satan knows that if you doubt your salvation, you'll never distinguish yourself in service. You cannot live in fear that you will lose your salvation and live in faith at the same time. Yet without faith it is impossible to please God (Hebrews 11:6). The spiritual vital signs in your life should dispel all doubt about your salvation.

If you're afraid that perhaps you are not saved, settle the issue once for all. Read the appendix included in this book. Get down on your knees right now, confess your sin, and ask the merciful God of heaven to save you from your sins through the faith you are expressing in Jesus' death at Calvary for you.

DISTANCE

If doubt doesn't get you, Satan will try distance. He'll say, "Okay, okay. So you're saved and sure of it. Go ahead and live anyway you want. You don't need God. Live to please yourself. Keep your distance from God, and He won't interfere in your life. You'll feel the exhilaration of freedom."

Can you imagine a starving man keeping his distance from the dinner table? Or a freezing man keeping his distance from a warm fire? That's absurd. But it's just as absurd once you entered a dynamic relationship with God to keep your distance from Him. When a hungry man keeps his distance from food, starvation wins. When a freezing man keeps his distance from the warmth of the fire, the cold wind wins. When you keep your distance from God, Satan wins.

That old devil will do whatever he can to keep you aloof from the Lord. He'll make sure the phone rings to interrupt your quiet time with God. He'll arrange for that big snowfall to come on Saturday night to keep you from church. Anything that will help you develop intimacy with God will be on Satan's hit list. Don't think finding a daily time for family devotions will be easy. Satan hates that about as much as anything. But if you want to feel the warmth of God, don't keep your distance. "Draw near to God and He will draw near to you" (James 4:8). Remember that the second secret to spiritual success is developing intimacy with God. Go ahead, disappoint Satan.

DEADLOCK

Choose a word. Impasse. Standstill. Stalemate. Deadlock. They all imply that you're going nowhere, and unless you've established good growth habits in your Christian life, that's where you're going—nowhere. Satan likes that. He much prefers spiritual deadlock to spiritual decline, because others will see decline and intercept it. When your friends at church see you backsliding, they may muster up enough courage to speak to you. But deadlock? No progress in your Christian life? No growth? Just nothing happening? Not many will challenge you about that, and Satan knows it. He's good at encouraging your spiritual status quo.

To learn the secrets to spiritual success, we have to learn to break out of the rut of spiritual infancy. We have to move on from milk to meat. We have to know when we've been at the entry level long enough and it's time to soar to what we once thought were unattainable heights of spiritual growth.

Are you ready to break the deadlock and grow? Are you ready to move to the next level of spiritual maturity? Are you ready to be the spiritual mentor rather than the spiritual mooch? If you are, you're ready to tackle one of the major secrets to spiritual success—establishing good growth habits. Do the right thing. Do what it takes to get growing.

DETACHMENT

Here's where the devil gets a lot of us. That old snake convinces us that we are strong, sufficient, better than average in intelligence, so we can grow and mature on our own. We can be spiritually successful without anyone's help. If it's a fight

Satan wants, it's a fight he'll get. We're ready for him, all by ourselves. We don't need any help.

Satan likes nothing better than the overconfidence of a Lone Ranger Christian. If we detach ourselves from the care and concern of other believers, we've done a big part of his work for him. He doesn't have to single us out the way a rustler separates a cow from the herd or a coyote singles out a sheep from the flock. We've done that by our fierce independence. A devilish smile breaks across Satan's face when he hears a Christian say things like, "I don't need a pastor; I don't need the church; I am everything I need to be spiritually successful." Much of our spiritual success depends on enlisting the right kind of help to assist us in our spiritual growth.

Larry and Rhonda had been active in their church for decades. She taught Sunday school; he served on the elder board and ushered. After a new pastor precipitated a major conflict, Larry and Rhonda left the church, stayed away for years, trying to grow in their Christian life simply by reading the Word and praying together on Sunday mornings at home. Without the support of fellow believers, however, their values shifted from church activities to a variety of worldly pursuits, including major involvement in gambling.

That's what happens when we become detached from other Christians and the local church. If you separate a hot coal from the rest of the coals, it soon becomes cold. But put it back with the others, and a cold coal becomes hot again. Why? Because each of us has some heat to give to others. If you fail to enlist the superior help of others, you fail to tap into one of God's great resources for your spiritual success.

DOMINANCE

If Satan can't keep us from salvation and can't make us the servant of doubt, he'll enslave us with some enticement. Temptation is one of Satan's most used tools because it's one of his most successful. It's his way of dominating us even though he cannot change our destiny. Unmanaged temptation keeps us safely tucked away in Satan's back pocket. He dominates us with our appetites and desires. He enslaves us with the people and things that inappropriately interest us.

Temptation is more than Satan's teaser. It's his way of controlling God's possessions. Temptation is not sin, but it's got Satan's fingerprints all over it, and it will lead us to sin if we fail to manage it. Our subtle tempter throws enticements at us right and left, big and little. The road to spiritual success must necessarily blast its way through temptation. We cannot avoid it, but we can defeat it.

Dominance through temptation, even the tiniest temptation, takes the joy out of Christian living and robs us of spiritual success. But God will help you manage temptation if you ask Him. John Bunyan, author of *Pilgrim's Progress,* admitted, "Temptation provokes me to look upward to God." When you're feeling a bit helpless in temptation management, look upward. Deliverance is just a prayer away.

DEFAULT

But what if we fail to pray and aren't delivered from temptation? What if we give in to those people or things that tempt us? What then? Is our Christian life a wipeout? Is heaven out of the question? No, not at all. But if we want to feel good about how we have lived and served the Savior, we have to retake the strongholds that have fallen through temptation. We cannot default on our responsibility to get up from the battlefield and fight again. If we do, we are the loser and Satan the winner.

One of the secrets to spiritual success is recognizing, as that great theologian Yogi Berra once said, that "it ain't over, till it's over." You may have stumbled and fallen. You may not have enjoyed spiritual success as you hoped when you were a young Christian. So what? Are you dead? Are all your opportunities to grab spiritual success gone? Look around you. If you are alive, there is hope. Those who have enjoyed spiritual success in this life have been down, too, but they got back up. They retook their strongholds. They foiled Satan's schemes and trusted the promises of God. The end result? They proved one of the secrets to spiritual success. You can be spiritually successful, too, but only if you don't default on battling Satan. He'll steal the joy of your salvation from you if you let him. It's up to you.

DISTRACTION

Satan is extremely gifted in employing the tactics represented by the six words we've just mentioned. The most subtle, however, is undoubtedly the last—distraction. To rob us of spiritual success, all Satan has to do is distract us from eternal things. If he can get us to live for the present, spend for the present, and plan for the present, he will rob us of the future.

Do you want to know if you've been distracted by your arch enemy? There's an easy way to find out. Compare what you did today that will disappear in time with what you did that will last for eternity. Chart your activities for this past week. How many of them changed people's lives? How many of them would you take the time to do again if you knew you had just one more week on earth? Be honest.

Boot up your computer or take out your checkbook and take a look at your personal financial program. Where did most of your money go this past year? What did you invest in that will last forever and what did you spend that is already gone? Is distraction a problem for you? A hundred years from now, will you be happy at the way your spent your time, your money, your life, or will Satan be happy?

Is it time for a life inventory? Hard issues require hard questions, and much of your spiritual success will depend on how you answer the hard questions. In your life, who's ahead—you or Lucifer? Which one of you had a better day today? Which one will have a better day tomorrow?

Spiritual secrets are only secrets to those unaware of them. But once we're aware, they are only useful to those who practice them. The seven secrets to spiritual success aren't magic, but they are prudent. And best of all, they work. Let them be secrets no more; let them be your steps to spiritual success.

SPIRITUAL SUCCESS IS WITHIN YOUR GRASP

I've been on my personal spiritual journey for a long time. Like you, I've had my ups and downs. Like you, I've had my spiritual successes and failures. But I have learned one truth more consistently than any other along the way: God wants us to succeed. God wants us to be spiritually successful, and He has given us everything we need to be successful.

- He has given us an understandable manual for success—the Bible. "This Book of the Law shall not depart from your mouth, but you shall meditate in it day and night, that you may observe to do according to all that is written in it. For then you will make your way prosperous, and then you will have good success" (Joshua 1:8).
- He has given us the power to energize us for success—the Holy Spirit. "You are of God, little children, and have overcome them, because He who is in you is greater than he who is in the world" (1 John 4:4).
- He has given us the goal for success—Jesus Christ. "That I may know Him and the power of His resurrection, and the fellowship of His sufferings, being conformed to His death" (Philippians 3:10).
- He has given us His promise—victory. "Yet in all these things we are more than conquerors through Him who loved us" (Romans 8:37).

Spiritual success is not a pipe dream; with all you have going for you, it's within your grasp.

As a fellow pilgrim, I wish you well on your journey. I thank you for taking the time to think with me about the seven secrets that will bring spiritual success to you. And I encourage you to share this book and these secrets with others you care about. After all, we're on the winning side, so there's no reason to be lonely on the road to heaven.

I'll see you on the road.

APPENDIX

HOW TO KNOW YOU ARE SAVED

Christians want to know they're going to heaven when they die, and they want to know for sure. But is that possible? Can we really know beyond doubt that we're on our way to heaven? Or must we hesitantly stumble through life playing a guessing game?

Frankly, those who aren't absolutely certain of their salvation suffer from a pretty anemic Christian life. It's not that they don't walk with the Lord; they do. But their walk is under a constant rain cloud. They don't have the joy that Jesus intended to be a part of an intrepid relationship with Him. They don't experience spiritual growth as rapidly as they could because they are continually struggling with the cancer of doubt.

Besides, if they're not sure they're going to heaven, how can they tell someone else how to get there? A gnawing concern about assurance not only destroys the joy of their own salvation, it also destroys their effectiveness as witnesses. That's a shame, because such gnawing doubts are not necessary.

Most people lack assurance of salvation for two reasons. First, they do not understand the basis of their salvation. Second, they do not appreciate the means of their salvation. If you get God's perspective on these issues, you'll have far fewer doubts and far more assurance of your eternal destination.

THE DEMONS OF DOUBT

Let's investigate these demons of doubt. I call them demons because they are tools of the devil himself. Since Satan can't keep you from becoming a new creature in

Christ, he pesters you with doubt about your salvation. As you read the next pages, do a spiritual self-examination. Ask yourself if Satan is using these demons to cause you to doubt your salvation and keep you powerless and ineffective as a Christian.

Most people lack assurance of their salvation because they lack understanding. They do not appreciate what God's Word says about the basis or the means of their salvation. They have a skewed view of why and how they can be saved, and that view causes them to doubt. If we have a correct view of our salvation, doubt will be forced from our minds. Here's what the Bible says about the way we are saved.

THE BASIS OF SALVATION

On what grounds does God save us? If God is holy and just, how can He save admittedly sinful people like you and me and still be true to His character? What is the basis of our salvation?

When the rich young ruler came to Jesus and asked, "Good Teacher, what shall I do that I may inherit eternal life?" (Mark 10:17), he was asking the same question we are asking. What is the basis of our salvation? When the Philippian jailer asked Paul and Silas, "Sirs, what must I do to be saved?" (Acts 16:30), he was asking our question. When an expert in the law asked Jesus, "Teacher, what shall I do to inherit eternal life?" (Luke 10:25), he was asking the same thing. And when Paul Fordyce, who owns an automobile dealership in Virginia, asked me, "How can God possibly save me after the things I've done in my life?" he was asking the timeless question: What is the basis of our salvation?

So how should we answer the question? What is the basis of our salvation? Is it the old idea that your "good deeds will one day outweigh your bad deeds and tip the scales in your favor" an accurate picture of salvation? That's a pretty risky possibility. Scary, too.

IT'S A DONE DEAL

There is nothing we can do to merit God's redemption. The good deeds/bad deeds idea is a common misconception. Notice that each one who asked the question above thought it was something he could do that would bring salvation. But the basis of our salvation is not what we do; it's what Jesus Christ did for us at Calvary's cross. Our salvation is grounded in the substitutionary death of Jesus Christ for our sins—nothing more, nothing less. That means the basis of salvation is beyond our control. We can't change it, challenge it, or contribute to it. It's out of our hands.

I remember when the great Michael Jordan said he would retire, but many didn't believe it. After all, he had retired before, then came back to play basketball. Besides, how else could he make over thirty million dollars a year playing the game he loved? Throughout the summer of 1998, however, Jordan said he planned to retire, and those closest to him said the same thing. The rest of the league and basketball fans around the country watched and waited. Finally, in January 1999, after a lengthy NBA strike was settled, Jordan called a press conference at the United Center in Chicago. He confirmed in January what he had said the previous summer: His retirement was a done deal. Jordan followed through on what he said he'd do, even though many people doubted him.

That's the way it is with our salvation. Despite our doubts, God has followed through on His plan. Jesus died on the cross for us. His blood paid the penalty for our sins. He appeased the wrath of God. He offered Himself up as a perfect sacrifice for us. Once the Calvary event was over, salvation was a done deal. All we have to do is accept what He did for us at Calvary's cross, and it's a done deal for us, too.

Since Jesus' death is the sole basis of our salvation, that begs several questions: Why Jesus and not someone else? What happened when Jesus died? How does what He did at Calvary impact your ability to know for sure you are saved? Let's think about both the principles and proofs of the basis of salvation.

JESUS WAS OUR SACRIFICE

God has always demanded a blood sacrifice for sin. "It is the blood that makes atonement for the soul" (Leviticus 17:11). Some snicker at it, but God doesn't take sin lightly. He is too holy to look the other way when we sin and too just to sweep our sin under the cosmic rug. Habakkuk 1:13 says of God, "You are of purer eyes than to behold evil, and cannot look on wickedness." That's a real problem for sinners like you and me.

Here's the principle. God is sinless and we are sinful. The only way we can enjoy the presence of a sinless God is to be sinless, too. But that's impossible. How can we do anything that would satisfy the demands of God to be sinless? In fact, we can't, but He can. God Himself provided a sacrifice to meet His own demands. That's what He did at Mount Moriah for Abraham and Isaac (Genesis 22:1–14). And that's what He did at Mount Calvary for you and me. God atoned for our sin by providing His own sacrifice—His one and only Son, Jesus Christ. Jesus bled and died as a sacrifice to make atonement for us because "without shedding of blood there is no remission" or payment for our sin (Hebrews 9:22).

Here's the proof. The Bible says that Jesus "was delivered up because of our offenses" (Romans 4:25). "Delivered up" means to hand over as the court would hand over a guilty person to be executed. It's the same word that's used in Ephesians 5:2 of Christ who "has loved us and given Himself for us, an offering and a sacrifice to God." God gave up His own Son at Calvary to be the sacrifice He Himself required to pay for your sin.

JESUS WAS OUR SUBSTITUTE

We are saved on the basis that Jesus was an acceptable sacrifice for our sins. But that begs other questions: Why didn't God just let us die for our own sins? Why substitute Jesus' life for our life? The answer is simple. We were incapable of providing an acceptable sacrifice.

God has always demanded a blood sacrifice for sin, and that sacrifice had to be perfect, without any moral or ethical flaw. You and I just didn't fit the bill. Sin has permeated us as completely as if it were an Ebola virus. So God provided His own Son to be the sacrifice for us. He loved us that much!

Here's the principle. Since we are not capable of being our own sacrifice, we needed a sinless substitute. In the eternal and infinite wisdom of the Godhead, it was determined that Jesus, God the Son, would come to earth to become a man, remain entirely sinless, and offer Himself as our substitute. If Jesus had not made Himself available to be our substitute, we would have no hope of salvation, let alone hope of assurance. But Jesus willingly took upon Himself the pain of our sin and became our substitutionary sacrifice. As Bernard of Clairvaux noted in the Medieval Latin poem that was later set to music in the hymn "O Sacred Head, Now Wounded": "What Thou, my Lord, hast suffered was all for sinners' gain; mine, mine was the transgression, but Thine the deadly pain."

Here's the proof. The Bible says that Jesus "bore our sins in His own body on the tree, that we, having died to sins, might live for righteousness" (1 Peter 2:24). Jesus did not die at Calvary because He was guilty; He died because *we* were guilty. He substituted Himself for us. Paul says that God the Father "made Him who knew no sin to be sin for us, that we might become the righteousness of God in Him" (2 Corinthians 5:21). Jesus went to the cross in perfect righteousness and shouldered the burden of your sin, my sin, and the sin of the whole world. Now you and I can stand before God clothed in Christ's righteousness instead of the nakedness of our own sinfulness.

Read Hebrews 9 and you'll become convinced that the basis of your salvation is solely in Christ's substitutionary sacrifice at Calvary. He "obtained eternal redemption" (v.12) for you when He "offered Himself without spot to God" (v. 14), so that by "the blood of Christ" (v. 14), He has "put away sin by the sacrifice of Himself" (v. 26). Jesus alone is our sacrifice because He alone could be our substitute.

JESUS IS OUR SAVIOR

The Bible does not leave any room for "adjustive interpretation" here. It's right there in black and white. The basis of our salvation is not what we think, what we do, or who we are. It is solely Jesus' substitutionary sacrifice at Calvary's cross that provides for our salvation.

Here's the principle. Jesus was always God, but it was His work at Calvary that made Him the Savior. Do you remember what the angel told the shepherds on the night Jesus came to earth? "For there is born to you this day in the city of David a Savior, who is Christ the Lord" (Luke 2:11). The cross is why He came. You are why He came.

It is not His person that makes Jesus the Lamb of God. It is His work at Calvary. Even when John the Baptist pointed to Jesus and said, "Behold! The Lamb of God who takes away the sin of the world!" (John 1:29), he was reflecting his belief that Jesus would soon be keeping His appointment with destiny at Calvary.

Here's the proof. The Bible says the atoning work of Christ was confined to what He accomplished on the cross. Paul said it in Colossians 1:19–20 this way: "For it pleased the Father that in Him all the fullness should dwell, and by Him to reconcile all things to Himself, by Him, whether things on earth or things in heaven, having made peace through the blood of His cross." Jesus' sinless life, His obedience to the Father, His deity, and His perfect humanity all demonstrated that He was worthy to be the Savior, but these did not make Him the Savior. Only His death at Calvary accomplished our redemption (Isaiah 53:10; Hebrews 9:12–14). When the sinless, substitutionary sacrifice died, He became the Savior of the world.

The focal point of salvation is the cross. The basis of our salvation is the cross. Because of what Jesus did at the cross, you and I have the opportunity to be saved and have assurance of our salvation. If you fail to understand the necessity of the cross, you will fail to appreciate the foundation of your salvation, and you will constantly worry about whether or not you have done enough to please God.

THE MEANS OF SALVATION

If you understand the basis of your salvation, you have swung the bat, hit the ball, and run to first. You're on base, but you aren't home yet.

How was Jesus' sacrifice applied to us? How did His death give us life? God sprung the Hebrews from Egyptian bondage in a most unusual way. That fateful Passover night, they were told to take a lamb and sacrifice it for their family (Exodus 12:21). That was the basis of their Passover deliverance.

The blood from the slain lamb was collected in a bowl. But just collecting the lamb's blood was insufficient to save the Jews that night. It wasn't until the blood was placed on the lintel and the doorposts of the house that the angel of the Lord passed over the home and spared the family. The blood had to be applied to be effective. The means of salvation was just as important as the basis of salvation.

What is the means of your salvation, and how does the way you are saved provide vital signs of spiritual life? Those are legitimate questions, and they are interrelated. When people ask how they can be saved, they are not asking about the basis of salvation. They are asking about its means. Their real question is, "By what means can I be saved?"

A MATTER OF FAITH

We have already noted that what we do makes no contribution to our salvation. When the Philippian jailer asked Paul, "What must I do to be saved?" Paul didn't say, "Try to live a good life, and I'm sure God will be pleased." No, the apostle replied, "Believe on the Lord Jesus Christ, and you will be saved" (Acts 16:31). Salvation is a matter of believing that what Jesus did on the cross is all that we need to be saved. We can't add to what He did, but we can reject what He did. So what does it mean to believe in the Lord Jesus?

To trust Jesus Christ as Savior requires faith that consists of three elements: assent, repentance, and trust. These are the qualities that make faith salvational faith. You can't do anything to be saved, but when you express true faith, it will encompass these ingredients.

ASSENT TO THE FACTS OF THE GOSPEL

The gospel is good news, but so are a lot of other things. To New Yorkers, the Yankees winning the World Series is also good news. So what makes the good news of the gospel so special? Just this: The facts of the gospel address man's desperate spiritual need, God's gracious provision in Christ to meet that need, and how we must respond if we are to be saved. If we do not acknowledge these truths when we believe, we do not have the kind of faith that saves.

Once I was about to conduct a funeral, and the funeral director and I were chatting in the back room before the service began. He attended a liberal church, and he said to me, "Most people miss what Christianity is all about. It's not hell and damnation. It's love. God is good, and He loves us." I agreed that God loves us, but added, "People need to know there is bad news before they can appreciate there is good news."

Before we can believe anything else, we must understand that we all have rebelled against God, and that is sin (Genesis 3:1–6). Each new generation is sinful by birth (Psalm 51:5; Job 14:4), by imputation (Romans 5:12–21), and by choice (2 Samuel 12:13; Job 7:20; Micah 7:9; Matthew 27:4; Luke 15:21). As a result we are all spiritually dead, stillborn in our relationship with God (Genesis 2:17; Ephesians 2:1), without hope and destined for eternal hell (Ephesians 2:11–13). Understanding that this is true, even if we don't fully comprehend all the implications, is a necessary part of believing the gospel.

Beyond this, we must understand that, even though we have been rebellious toward God and are therefore condemned sinners (Ezekiel 18:4, 20; Romans

6:23), God nevertheless loves us dearly. That's part of the good news. While we were sinning, God was loving (Romans 5:6–8). He has made provision for our salvation through Christ's atonement (2 Corinthians 5:21).

There's more. God has a plan for reconciling us to Himself (2 Corinthians 5:18–19). It's His plan of salvation, and it called for God the Son, Jesus Christ, to come to earth and die as our sacrifice, our substitute, and our Savior. That's the basis of our salvation. When we recognize that Jesus Christ is God's only way to salvation (John 14:6), that He and He alone can justify us before God (Romans 3:23–24), and that there is only one name and one Person who can provide eternal life (Acts 4:12), then we have understood the basic facts that comprise God's good news. We have given assent to the essential facts of the gospel. But knowing how to be saved doesn't make us saved. Even the demons know how. Something more is needed.

REPENTANCE OF SIN

Repentance means a change of mind and attitude toward God and what His Word says. When you give mental assent to the facts of the gospel, something happens in your mind and your heart. That's repentance. You were rebellious toward God, indifferent or even hostile toward what the Bible says about salvation. But saving faith is accompanied with a change of mind, or it isn't the kind of faith that saves.

Repentance is not something tacked on to faith. It is not a "work" done either before or after you trust Christ. It's the flip side of being converted, of turning to Christ in faith. If faith is giving mental assent to the facts of the gospel—that you are a sinner and Jesus alone can be your Savior—then repentance is what you turn from when you turn to Christ. Millard J. Erickson explains it this way:

> Conversion is a single entity which has two distinguishable but inseparate aspects; repentance and faith. Repentance is the unbeliever's turning away from sin, and faith is his or her turning toward Christ. They are, respectively, the negative and positive aspect of the same occurrence. In a sense, each is incomplete without the other, and each is motivated by the other. As we become aware of sin and turn from it, we see the necessity of turning to Christ for the provision of his righteousness. Conversely, believing in Christ makes us aware of our sin and thus leads to repentance."[1]

In some respects, coming to Christ is like beginning a new year. The old year is gone forever and will never be back. The new year has dawned. The day you believe on the Lord Jesus Christ is like January 1. The month of January is named after Janus, the Roman god that is identified with doors, gates, and all beginnings. He is represented as having two faces, looking in opposite directions.

Repenting of sin and placing your faith in Jesus Christ as Savior is the door to new life, eternal life (John 10:9). The difference between Janus and the Christian is that we aren't looking back. Repentance means you are no longer looking back into the old year (or the old life), but you are turning from that life to look confidently into your new life in Christ. "Therefore, if anyone is in Christ, he is a new creation; old things have passed away; behold, all things have become new" (2 Corinthians 5:17).

FAITH IN CHRIST AS SAVIOR

There is one final ingredient to the gospel that ties it all together. Assent to the facts and repentance from sin must be accompanied by genuine faith in Jesus Christ as your Savior. Giving mental assent to these facts is much more than acknowledging their existence; it is acknowledging their absolute truthfulness. We do not take a nonrational leap into the dark when we believe on the Lord Jesus Christ. We believe the facts as God presents them in His Word, and we believe those facts apply to us. This is not a jump into some paranormal black hole; it is an acknowledgment that God's Word is true (John 17:17) and a con- scious embracing of what God says about Jesus and His atoning work (2 Timothy 3:14–15; 1 Peter 1:23–25).

You cannot do this without help. After all, you are spiritually stillborn, dis- tant from God and not interested in the facts of the gospel. But when the Spirit of God draws you to the Father (John 6:44) and enlightens your mind, He makes it possible for you to believe the facts of the gospel (1 Corinthians 2:14). When that happens you say, "It finally makes sense to me. What the Bible says really is true." That's more than mental assent and repentance—that's faith! Without faith it is impossible to please God (Hebrews 11:6).

FAITH PLUS NOTHING

When Paul told the Philippian jailer, "Believe on the Lord Jesus Christ and you will be saved," he meant believe in such a way that you admit what God says about you is true; believe in such a way that you turn from the past, confidently look toward the future, and personally trust Christ and Christ alone as all you need to be your Savior. Having believed that, what else does God require of you for salvation? Nothing!

While there are some who link baptism to salvation as a requirement, the preponderance of texts speak of baptism as a token of salvation, not a requisite for it (Matthew 28:19–20). Belief followed by baptism is the pattern in Acts 8:12; 18:8, and 19:1–7.

If you're concerned about whether or not you are saved, ask yourself these questions:

Do you trust what God said in His Word that you are a sinner?
Do you believe that God gave His Son to die in your place to atone for your sin?
Do you believe Jesus Christ is the only Savior this world will ever have?
Do you believe that you cannot do anything to be saved, but you must believe that what Jesus did for you is all you need to be saved?

Those are the facts of the gospel, and if you believe these facts, do you believe them in a way that makes you want to turn from your sinful past and accept His glorious future?

NO BETTER TIME

One final thing. Has there ever been a time in your life when you actually asked Jesus Christ to be your Savior? If the answer is yes, the issue is closed. You are saved, born again, born from above by the grace of God.

If the answer is no, there is no better time than right now to make the answer yes. Admit your sin and need for a Savior. Believe what Jesus did when He died for you on the cross is all you need to be saved. Ask Him to save you. If you genuinely mean it, He will. He really will.

NOTES

PREFACE: LAUNCHING OUT ON THE JOURNEY

1. The first manned Apollo flight, scheduled for February 1967, was delayed when on January 27, 1967, during a countdown rehearsal, a fire broke out inside the spacecraft cabin and spread rapidly, killing three astronauts: Virgil "Gus" Grissom, Edward White, and Roger Chaffee.

SPIRITUAL SECRET #1: CHECK FOR VITAL SIGNS

1. C. S. Lewis, *Surprised by Joy* (San Diego: Harcourt Brace Jovanovich, Publishers, 1955), 229.

2. Oswald Chambers, *My Utmost for His Highest* (New York: Dodd, Mead and Company, 1935), 284.

3. Wayne Grudem, *Systematic Theology* (Grand Rapids: Zondervan Publishing House, 1994), 803–6.

SPIRITUAL SECRET #2: DEVELOP INTIMACY WITH GOD

1. A. W. Tozer, *The Pursuit of God* (Camp Hill, Penn.: Christian Publications, Inc., 1982), 15.

2. Douglas Kelly and Philip Rollinson, *The Westminster Shorter Catechism in Modern English* (Phillipsburg, N.J.: Presbyterian and Reformed Publishing Co., 1986), 5.

3. John Piper, *Desiring God* (Portland, Ore.: Multnomah Press, 1986), 18.

4. Cynthia Thomas, "Discipleship" in the "To Illustrate" column, *Leadership* (Winter 1994).

5. C. H. Faust and T. H. Johnson, eds., "Personal Narrative" in *Jonathan Edwards* (New York: Hill and Wang, 1962), 61.

6. Henry T. Blackaby and Claude V. King, *Experiencing God* (Nashville: Broadman and Holman Publishers, 1994), 34–5.

7. Tozer, *The Pursuit of God*, 12.

8. Blackaby and King, *Experiencing God*, 19.

9. A. W. Tozer, *The Knowledge of the Holy* (New York: Harper and Row, Publishers, 1961), 6.

SPIRITUAL SECRET #3: ESTABLISH GOOD GROWTH HABITS

1. *U.S. News and World Report*, 10 November 1997, 96.

2. John Wilson, "The Living Bible Reborn," *Christianity Today*, 28 October 1996, 35.

3. David F. Wells, *No Place for Truth* (Grand Rapids: William B. Eerdmans Publishing Company, 1993), 107–8.

4. J. I. Packer, Foreword in R. C. Sproul's, *Knowing Scripture* (Downers Grove, Ill.: Tyndale House Publishers, Inc., 1977).

5. John MacArthur, *Keys to Spiritual Growth* (Old Tappan, N.J.: Revell, 1978), 19.

6. George Gallup Jr. and Sarah Jones, *100 Questions and Answers: Religion in America* (Princeton: Princeton Religion Research Center, 1989), 39.

7. Dallas Willard, *The Spirit of the Disciplines* (San Francisco: Harper and Row, 1988), 186.

8. Theodore Roosevelt, *Day-by-Day with Billy Graham*, edited and compiled by Joan Winmill Brown, (Minneapolis: World Wide Publications, 1976), reading for February 5.

9. "Spiritual America," *U.S. News and World Report*, 4 April 1994, 56.

10. Robert W. Patterson, "In Search of the Visible Church," *Christianity Today*, 11 March 1991, 36.

11. Warren Mueller, *Leadership* 2, no. 3, (1981).

12. Claudia Wallis, "Faith and Healing," *Time*, 24 June 1996, 60.

13. Win Arn, *The Master's Plan for Making Disciples* (Monrovia, Calif.: Church Growth Press, 1982), 43.

14. If you want to learn more about prayer, here's a helpful resource: Woodrow Kroll, *When God Doesn't Answer: Removing Roadblocks to Answered Prayer* (Grand Rapids: Baker Books, 1997).

SPIRITUAL SECRET #4: ENLIST SUPERIOR HELP

1. "Friends for Life," *Lincoln Journal Star,* 28 September 1995.

2. Charles Colson, *Kingdoms in Conflict* (Grand Rapids: Zondervan Publishing Company, 1981), 282.

3. Leslie B. Flynn, *Great Church Fights* (Wheaton, Ill.: Victor Books, 1976), 9.

4. Daniel Goleman, "Studies Shed Light on How Stress Erodes Health," *Courier Journal,* 8 February 1995.

5. Linda Phillips-Jones, *Mentors and Proteges* (New York: Arbor House, 1982), 37.

6. Charles R. Swindoll, *Flying Closer to the Flame* (Dallas: Word Publishing, 1993), 150.

7. Brad Scott in "First Person," *Moody Monthly*, September/October 1998, 84. Brad Scott has written a book about his experiences entitled *Embraced by the Darkness: Exposing New Age Theology* (Crossway Books, 1996).

SPIRITUAL SECRET #5: LEARN TO MANAGE TEMPTATION

1. The word *temptation (peirasmos)* is used two ways in the Bible. One meaning refers to adversity, affliction, or trial. This is the way Jesus used the word in Luke 22:28, when He said the disciples had continued with Him in His trials. It's

what Peter had in mind when he warned, "Beloved, do not think it strange concerning the fiery trial which is to try you" (1 Peter 4:12) or when James urged "My brethren, count it all joy when you fall into various trials" (1:2). See also Luke 8:13; Acts 20:19; James 1:12, and 2 Peter 2:9. The second meaning of *peirasmos* is enticement to sin. This seems to be the meaning of the word in Matthew 6:13; 26:41; Mark 14:38; Luke 4:13; 22:40, 46; 1 Corinthians 10:13; Galatians 4:14; and 1 Timothy 6:9.

2. "How Common Is Pastoral Indiscretion?" *Leadership* 2, no. 3, (Winter 1988): 12.

3. Quoted by R. Kent Hughes, *Disciplines of a Godly Man* (Wheaton, Ill.: Crossway Books, 1991), 264.

4. For a fuller treatment of how to plan your defense when you are tempted, see the advice of Jerry Kirk on how the traveling man can avoid falling to the temptation of pornography in the book *Seven Promises of a Promise Keeper* (Focus on the Family Publishing, 1999).

5. Quoted in Richard J. Foster and James Bryan Smith, eds., *Devotional Classics* (San Francisco: HarperSanFrancisco, 1992), 185.

6. See Woodrow Kroll and Don Hawkins, *Prodigal People* (Grand Rapids: Kregel Publications, 1995), 117–31.

7. Millard J. Erickson, *Introducing Christian Doctrine* (Grand Rapids: Baker Book House, 1992), 267.

SPIRITUAL SECRET #6: IF YOU FALL, DON'T STAY DOWN

1. *Webster's Ninth New Collegiate Dictionary* (Springfield, Mass: Merriam-Webster Inc., Publishers, 1991).

2. Bruce Weible, "Professional Con Artist's Luck Runs Out," *Lincoln Journal Star,* 14 February 1995.

3. Gordon MacDonald, *Rebuilding Your Broken World* (Nashville: Oliver Nelson, 1988), 165–6.

SPIRITUAL SECRET #7: KEEP YOUR EYE ON THE GOAL

1. Lewis Carroll, *Alice in Wonderland* (New York: Alfred A. Knopf, 1987), 72.

2. G. K. Chesterton, *Orthodoxy* (Chicago: Thomas More Association, 1985), 99–100.

3. Joseph M. Stowell, *Eternity* (Chicago: Moody Press, 1995), 243.

4. C. S. Lewis, *Mere Christianity* (New York: Macmillan, 1943), 118.

5. Woodrow Kroll, *Tested by Fire* (Neptune, N.J.: Loizeaux Brothers, 1977), 9-10.

6. Steven R. Covey, *The 7 Habits of Highly Effective People* (New York: Simon and Schuster, 1989), 98.

7. For a complete discussion of the criteria that will be used to judge us at

the judgment seat of Christ, see chapter 5 in *Tested by Fire*.

8. *San Francisco Examiner,* 3 May 1995.

9. The Associated Press, 4 February 1991.

10. Covey, *The 7 Habits of Highly Effective People,* 106.

11. Jack Canfield and Mark Hansen, *Chicken Soup for the Soul* (Deerfield Beach, Fla.: Health Communications, 1993), 191.

12. Lewis, *Mere Christianity,* 119.

APPENDIX: HOW TO KNOW YOU ARE SAVED

1. Millard J. Erickson, *Introducing Christian Doctrine* (Grand Rapids: Baker Books, 1992), 296.